Read

- Descriptions in this mar Microsoft Surface Pro/Microsoft Surface Laptop.

- All information supplied in this guide is for educational purpose only and users bear the responsibility for using it.

- All information supplied in this guide is what is available as at the time of writing this guide, and it may not be 100% accurate again if there is a major firmware/software update to Surface Laptop/All New Microsoft Surface Pro (2017 Model).

- Although I took tremendous effort to ensure that all information provided in this guide are correct, I will welcome your suggestions if you find out that any information provided in this guide is inadequate or you find a better way of doing some of the actions mentioned in this guide. All correspondence should be sent to pharmibrahimguides@gmail.com

Copyright and Trademarks

Microsoft Surface Pro and Microsoft Surface Laptop are trademarks of Microsoft, Inc. All other trademarks are the property of their respective owners. Reproduction of this book without the permission of the owner is illegal. Any request for permission should be directed to **pharmibrahimguides@gmail.com**.

Copyright © 2017 by Pharm Ibrahim

About This Guide

Finally, the Definitive Beginner's Guide on All-New Microsoft Surface Pro (2017 Edition) and Microsoft Surface Laptop Is Here!

This guide is a splendid companion for both All-New Microsoft Surface Pro (2017 Edition) and Microsoft Surface Laptop. It is a very thorough, no-nonsense guide, useful for both experts and newbies.

This guide contains a lot of information on Microsoft Surface Pro and Microsoft Surface Laptop.

It is full of actionable steps, hints, notes, screenshots and suggestions. This guide is particularly useful for newbies and seniors; nevertheless, I strongly believe that even the techy guys will find some benefits reading it.

Enjoy yourself as you go through this very comprehensive guide.

PS: Please make sure you don't give the gift of Microsoft Surface Pro or Microsoft Surface Laptop without giving this companion guide alongside with it. This guide makes your gift a complete one.

Table of Contents

How to Use This Guide (Please Read!)

This guide is an unofficial manual of Microsoft Surface Pro and Microsoft Surface Laptop and it should be used just like you use any reference book or manual.

To quickly find a topic, please use the table of contents. In addition, you can press **Ctrl + F** to search for any word or phrase in this guide. This will allow you to quickly find information and save time.

When I say you should press any key combination, for example, when I say you should press **Ctrl + J** or just any other key, what I mean is that you should press and hold the Control Key (**Ctrl**) and then press **J** key. You can also press these two keys simultaneously, if you can.

In addition, when I say you should carry out a set of tasks, for example when I say you should click **All settings > System > Notifications & actions**, what I mean is that you should click on **All settings** and then click on **System**. And lastly, you should click on **Notifications & actions**.

Lastly, I have based most of the information contained in this guide on the assumption that you are going to be controlling your Microsoft Surface Pro/Microsoft Surface Laptop with the trackpad. However, you will still get similar result by using your finger or Surface pen to control the touchscreen. For example, when I instruct you to click an item using the trackpad, you will get a similar result if you click the item with a finger or Surface pen. In addition, if the instruction says you should right-click an item, you can also hold your finger down on the item to get similar results as you would get when you right-click.

I hope this guide helps you to get the most out of your Surface.

Getting Started With Your Microsoft Surface Pro and Microsoft Surface Laptop

Unpacking Your Device

When you unpack your product box, be sure that it contains the following items:

1. Microsoft Surface Pro/Microsoft Surface Laptop (depending on the one you bought);
2. Quick Start Guide; and
3. Charger.

In addition, if you are buying a new product, make sure that the product box is sealed when you receive your item.

Downside: Unlike Surface Pro 4 and Surface Book, Microsoft Surface Pro and Microsoft Surface Laptop don't come with Surface Pen. You will have to spend extra dollars to purchase one.

Charging your device

To charge your Microsoft Surface Pro/Microsoft Surface Laptop:

1. When you first open your product box, you will notice that the power adapter consists of two parts, connect these two parts together.

Connect the two parts of the power cord as shown

2. Connect the magnetic charging connector on the mouth of the power adapter to the charging port of your device, making sure that both the magnetic charging connector and the charging port on your device make a perfect contact.

Connect the magnetic charging connector to this port

3. Plug the power cord to an electrical outlet.

4. Check the power connector light. LED light on the power connector will turn on when your device is charging. In addition, the battery icon on the task bar will show a charging icon.

Please note that a light appears at the end of the connector when your Surface is getting power. If the battery level of your device is very low, there will be an alert screen prompting you to charge your device.

If you are using your Microsoft Surface Pro/Microsoft Surface Laptop more often (especially if you use wireless connection/LTE more often), you may realize that you need to charge your device more often. The best way to save the battery on your device is to put it on the **Airplane mode** or put it to sleep when not in use.

If you are using a Microsoft Surface Pro Type Cover with your Surface Pro, then please note that the Type Cover draws power from Surface Pro and this may make the battery on your Surface to drain faster.

Turning your Device on and off

To turn on your device, press the Power Key once. If you turn on your device for the first time, follow the on-screen instructions to set it up.

To turn off your Surface, click on ▦ (located at the left bottom corner of the screen) and then click ⏻ **Power.** Click **Shut Down.**

Alternatively, press and hold the power key and **slide down to power off.**

To restart your device, click on ▦ and then click **Power.** Click **Restart.**

If your device is not responding, press and hold the power button until your device goes off.

Please note that you may need to press and hold your device for more than 10 seconds before it goes off.

Note: It is advisable to charge your device before you set it up. However, if your device is fully charged when you received it, you may not need to charge it before using it.

Please note that using another power adapter (other than Microsoft charger) to charge your device may increase charging time.

Tip:

To avoid changing your device settings many times, make sure you choose those settings that you are most pleased with when you switch on your Surface for the first time.

Note: You will need a Microsoft account to fully setup your device. For example, you may need a Microsoft account to back up and restore your device, to buy, install, and update apps.

However, you can choose to create Microsoft account later. To create a Microsoft account at any time, click on and click **Settings**, click **Accounts** and then use the onscreen settings to setup, connect or disconnect from a Microsoft account.

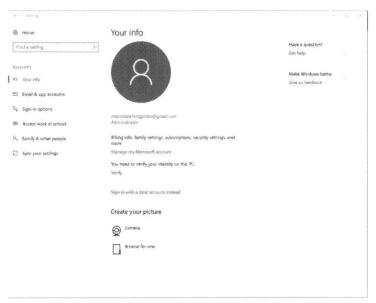

Get to know your device

Device Layout of All New Microsoft Surface Pro

Number	Function
1.	Mini DisplayPort
2.	USB 3.0 Port
3.	Charging Port

4.	Adjustable Kickstand
5.	Type Cover (Sold Separately)
6.	Back Camera
7.	Volume button
8.	Power Button
9.	Headset Jack Port
10.	Magnetic surface for Surface Pen
11.	Back Privacy Light
12.	Front Camera/Windows Hello Sign-In
13.	MicroSD Card Slot

Device Layout of Microsoft Surface Laptop

Number	Function
1.	Charging Port
2.	Power Button
3.	Front Camera/Windows Hello Sign-In
4.	Headset Jack Port
5.	Mini Display Port
6.	USB 3.0 Port

Inserting and Managing SD Card

The All New Microsoft Surface Pro (but not Microsoft Surface Laptop) supports the use of external memory card. Microsoft Surface Pro supports microSD card.

To insert memory card:

1. Insert the SD card into the SD card slot on your Surface, being careful to insert the card with the pins facing down. Please see page 6 and 7 for visual representation of the memory card slot of Surface Pro.

2. Check to see if the SD card is listed on your Surface. To do this, select the search box in the taskbar, enter **file explorer**, and in the search results, select **File Explorer**. Click on **This PC** and then look for the card.

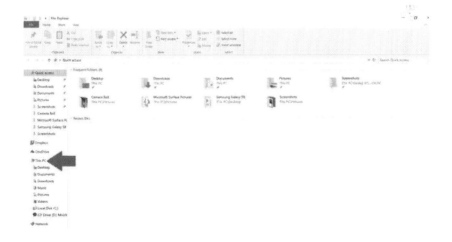

Notes: When purchasing a new memory card for your device, ensure that you are purchasing the right memory card (microSD card) to avoid unnecessary headaches.

Managing Your SD Card

You can manage how your Surface use your SD Card. You can choose what content is stored on memory card or Surface.

1. Click on > **All settings > System > Storage.**
2. To view more details on the storage type, click **This PC** or **SD Card.**
3. To change storage location on items, click on the drop-down box under the desired file types where you want to change, and then select **This PC** or **SD Card.** For example, to change the file location of documents, click the drop-down box under **New documents will save to:** and then select **This PC** or **SD Card** from the dialogue box that appears.

Note: *Please note that Microsoft Surface Laptop does not support MicroSD card.*

Transferring apps from your device to SD Card

You may consider transferring files from your Surface to your SD card in order to free up more space.

To transfer apps from internal storage to SD Card:

1. Click on 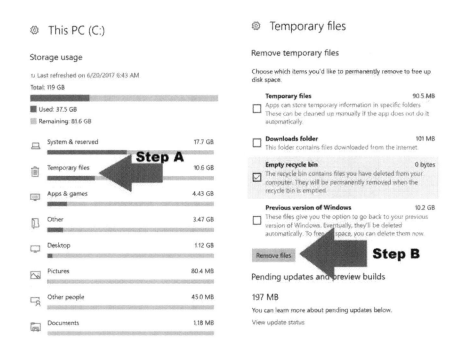 **> Settings > System > Storage > This PC > Apps & Games**.

2. Then Click the app you want to move, and Click **Move**.

Note: *You may not be able to move some apps on your Surface.*

Tip: You may consider removing temporary files from your device to free up space. To do this, swipe in from the right edge of the screen, click **All settings > System > Storage > This PC.** Click **Temporary files**, select all the files you want to delete and then tap **Remove files.**

This PC (C:)

Storage usage

ʊ Last refreshed on 6/20/2017 6:43 AM

Total: 119 GB

■ Used: 37.5 GB
▒ Remaining: 81.6 GB

💻	System & reserved	17.7 GB
🗑	Temporary files	10.6 GB
🖥	Apps & games	4.43 GB
📱	Other	3.47 GB
🖥	Desktop	1.12 GB
🖼	Pictures	80.4 MB
👥	Other people	45.0 MB
📄	Documents	1.18 MB

Step A

Temporary files

Remove temporary files

Choose which items you'd like to permanently remove to free up disk space.

☐ **Temporary files** 90.5 MB
Apps can store temporary information in specific folders. These can be cleaned up manually if the app does not do it automatically.

☐ **Downloads folder** 101 MB
This folder contains files downloaded from the internet.

☑ **Empty recycle bin** 0 bytes
The recycle bin contains files you have deleted from your computer. They will be permanently removed when the recycle bin is emptied.

☐ **Previous version of Windows** 10.2 GB
These files give you the option to go back to your previous version of Windows. Eventually, they'll be deleted automatically. To free up space, you can delete them now.

Remove files **Step B**

Pending updates and preview builds

197 MB

You can learn more about pending updates below.

View update status

Moving Your Items from Your Old PC to Your Surface

You can move your files to your new Surface by following one of the steps mentioned below:

- You can use a USB flash drive or a memory card to copy files from your old PC and then transfer them to your Surface.

 Please note that MicroSD cards work with All New Surface Pro while Surface Laptop does not support microSD cards.

- Add files to OneDrive app on your old system so that you can access them from your Surface. To move a file to OneDrive, just drag and drop the files to your OneDrive folder. The files will be uploaded to OneDrive cloud storage when you have an Internet connection on that computer. Once the files are on your OneDrive cloud storage, you can access them on your Surface by opening OneDrive app. To open OneDrive app, select the search box in the taskbar, enter **OneDrive**, and in the search results, tap **OneDrive**. To avoid any problem while trying to access your files, please ensure that you are connected to a network while trying to access OneDrive.

 You can also transfer items from your smartphones to your Surface using OneDrive. This is possible because there is OneDrive app for smartphones.

- Connect both old PC and your new Surface to the same network using Homegroup. To learn more about Homegroup, please refer to the section on **Connectivity** (please see page 250).

Using the touch screen

The touch screen of your Surface allows you to easily select items or perform functions.

Notes:

- Do not press the touch screen with your fingertips, or use sharp tools on the touch screen. Doing so may damage the touch screen or cause it to malfunction.
- Do not allow the touch screen to come into contact with other electrical appliances. This may cause the touch screen to malfunction.
- Do not allow the touch screen to come in contact with water. YOUR SURFACE IS NOT WATER RESISTANT. The touch screen may malfunction in humid conditions or when exposed to water.
- For optimal use of the screen, you may need to remove screen protector before using it. However, a good screen protector should be fully compatible and usable with your Surface.

You may control your touch screen with the following actions:

Tap: Touch once with your finger to select or launch a menu, application or option.

Tap and hold: Click an item and hold it for more than a second to open a list of options.

Tap and drag: Click and drag with your finger to move an item to a different location in the application grid/list.

Pinch: Place two fingers far apart, and then draw them closer together.

> **To Lock or Unlock the touch screen**

When you do not use the device for a specified period, your device turns off the touch screen and automatically locks the touch screen so as to prevent any unwanted device operations and also saves battery. To manually lock the touch screen, press the power key once.

To unlock, turn on the screen by pressing the power key and then swipe to unlock (or just press any key on the keyboard). If you have already set a lock screen password, you will be prompted to enter the password.

Rotating the touch screen

Your Surface has a built-in motion sensor that detects its orientation. If you rotate the device, the interface will automatically rotate according to the orientation. If you rotate your device horizontally, your device will change to Landscape mode, and if you rotate your device vertically, your device will enter Portrait mode.

Please note that the screen rotation may not work if your Surface is attached to the keyboard. In addition, please note that you may not be able to rotate the screen of your Surface Laptop.

➢ **Activating and deactivating screen rotation**

You may deactivate or activate screen rotation by following these steps:

1. To deactivate screen rotation, swipe in from the right edge of the screen to open the **ACTION CENTRE**, and click on **Rotation Lock** so that it becomes bold.

2. Alternatively, swipe in from the right edge of the screen to open the Action Center, click **All settings > System > Display** and then move the switch next to **Rotation Lock** to **On.**

Please note that the screen rotation option may not be available if the keyboard is attached to your Surface or if your Surface is not in **Tablet mode.** In addition, please note that you may not be able to rotate the screen of your Surface Laptop.

Getting to know Your Home/Start Screen

From your home screen, you can search for items and access applications. While on the start screen (or just any screen), swipe in from the right edge of the screen to open the Action Center.

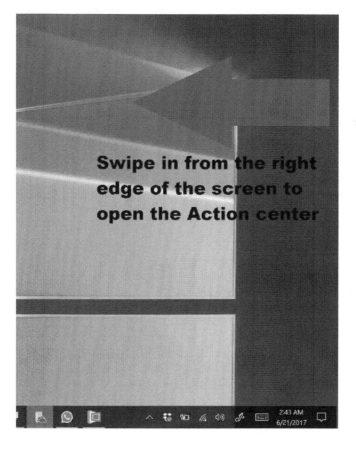

You can also quickly organize files by clicking and dragging one file on top of the other. In addition, you can move an app/file from one location to another on the start screen by clicking and dragging it.

Number	Function
1.	**Start/Windows Button**
2.	**Search menu**
3.	**Microphone icon**: Use this icon to access Cortana's feature
4.	**Task view icon**: Use this button to access all your open apps. Alternatively, swipe in from the left edge of the screen to access the Task view and see all your open apps.
5.	**Taskbar icons**: Click on any of these icons to launch it. You can pin an icon to the taskbar by right clicking on it and selecting **Pin to taskbar**. To rearrange the taskbar icons,

	double-tap an icon with a finger, then without releasing the icon, drag it to a new position. Alternatively, using the keyboard's trackpad, left click an icon with a finger and then use another finger to drag the icon to another location on the taskbar.
6.	Click on this caret icon to show hidden icons
7.	**Extra taskbar icons:** Click on any of these icons to launch it. To rearrange the taskbar icons, double-tap an icon with a finger, then without releasing the icon, drag it to a new position. Alternatively, using the keyboard's trackpad, left click an icon with a finger and then use another finger to drag the icon to another location on the taskbar.
8.	**Windows Ink Workspace icon**: Click this icon to manage sketchpad, sticky notes, pen settings and Windows Ink settings
9.	**On-Screen Keyboard Icon**
10.	**Action center icon**: Click on this to access the Action Center. Alternatively, swipe in from the right edge of the screen to access the action center.

Removing items/apps from the home/start screen

1. Click on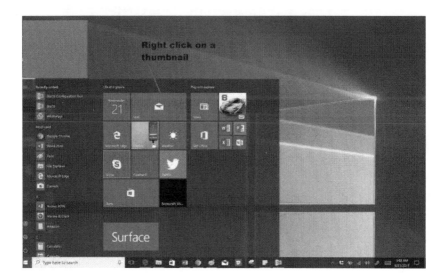

2. Right click on a thumbnail on the start screen and select **Unpin from Start.**

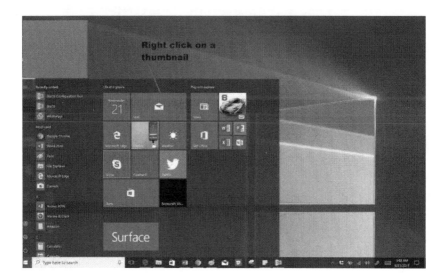

To uninstall an app:

1. Click on

2. Scroll down or up to find the app you want to uninstall.

3. Right click on an app and select **Uninstall** from the options that appear.

Right click an app

Selecting **Uninstall** will remove the app permanently from your device. Please note that your Surface comes preloaded with some apps and these preinstalled apps may not be removed.

To add an app to the tile screen:

Tile Screen

1. Click on

2. Scroll down or up to find the app you want to pin to tile screen.

3. Right click on an app and select **Pin to Start** from the options that appear.

To resize a tile:

1. Right click a tile and select **Resize**.

2. You can choose from **small, medium,** or **wide**.

Accessing Applications

1. Click on to access tiles and application list.

2. Click on the app of your choice

Tip: If you are using an app and you want to find additional settings and actions that are not shown as icons, click ☰ or ... (this two icons are usually located at the right upper corner and left lower corner part of the screen respectively.)

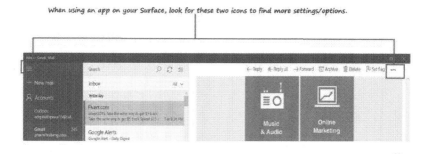

When using an app on your Surface, look for these two icons to find more settings/options.

Accessing Recently Opened or Running Applications

1. To access recent apps, click on ⊡ located on the task bar.
2. Alternatively, swipe in from the left side of the screen.
3. Click on an app to launch it, or click on the **X** icon to close it.
4. To create new desktop, tap + **New desktop**

Please note that each virtual desktop can have its own set of open apps. To switch between desktops, swipe in from the left side of the screen and select a desktop.

Select a desktop

Note: Although your Surface can run more than one app at the same time, multitasking may cause hang-ups, freezing, memory problems, or additional power consumption. To avoid these, end all unused apps by closing them.

Using the Taskbar

What is a taskbar?

Firstly, to be sure that everyone reading this guide knows what a taskbar is. I will quickly define it and follow it up with a screenshot. A taskbar is long horizontal bar containing a list of icons usually at the bottom of the screen.

It contains three sections namely:

- The start menu and search bar;
- The middle section containing opened, pinned apps and folders; and
- The notification area.

In addition, it is interesting to know that taskbar is not restricted to the bottom of the screen. It can also be moved to other parts of the screen like the right side or left side of the screen. To find out more, please go to page 29.

How do I setup multiple taskbar?

The most important thing to put at the back of one's mind when trying to set up multiple taskbars is that you will also need to setup multiple desktops. Your Surface comes with a feature that allows you to setup multiple desktops and that is why it is possible to have multiple taskbars.

So to setup multiple taskbar, you will need to setup a multiple desktop. To setup a multiple desktop, click on the task view icon 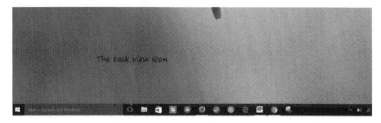 while on desktop mode. Alternatively, you can swipe in from the left edge of the screen.

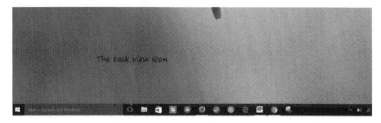

Then click on the + icon located at the right side of the screen. To create an additional desktop, click on the + icon again.

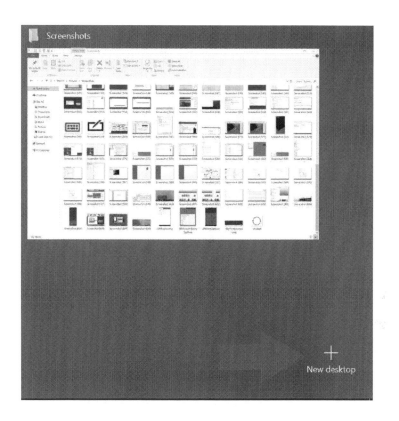

New desktop

After you have created multiple desktops, you would have automatically created multiple taskbars. Please note that not all applications support the multiple desktops or taskbars features. I expect Microsoft to increase the number of apps supporting this feature as time goes on.

To go to any of the taskbars, click on the task view icon and then click on the desktop thumbnail bearing the taskbar you want to access.

Note that if you pin an icon to any of the taskbars, it will also reflect on all other taskbars. However, if you open an application or folder on one taskbar, it will not reflect on other taskbars.

In addition, all the taskbars will contain the same start menu and notification area icons. It is only the middle section that will differentiate the taskbars.

Having multiple taskbars make it easy to multitask on your Surface device. It allows you to neatly sectionalize your work. Note that you can also rearrange the taskbar and put it at other sides of the screen. Please see the section below for more information.

How to Change the Taskbar Position or Rearrange the Taskbar on Your Surface Device

The taskbar on your device is located at the bottom of the screen by default. It is possible that you are not too convenient with the location and you may want to change the taskbar position.

To do this:

1. Right click an empty space on the taskbar (make sure you are not clicking any icon).

2. Then select **Taskbar settings**.

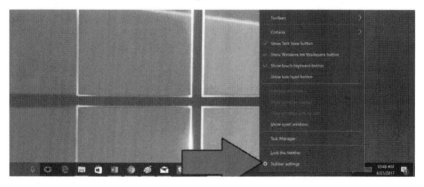

3. Click the dropdown box next to **Taskbar location on screen.** Then select your preferred location.

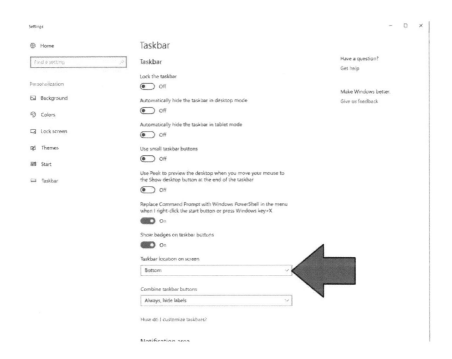

How to Rearrange Icons on the Taskbar

To rearrange icons on the taskbar:

1. To rearrange the taskbar icons, double-tap an icon with a finger, then without releasing the icon, drag it to a new position.

2.Alternatively, using the keyboard's trackpad, left click an icon with a finger and then use another finger to drag the icon to another location on the taskbar.

Step 2

Using this area of the trackpad, drag the icon to another part of the taskbar using another finger

Step 1

Left click and hold an icon using this part of the trackpad

How to remove icons from the taskbar

You can remove an icon from the taskbar by closing the application. If the application is already pinned to the taskbar then you will need to unpin it from the taskbar by following the instructions in the next section.

How to Hide Application from Taskbar

There are two ways to hide application from taskbar. The first one is to unpin the application icon from the taskbar if it is already pinned to the taskbar. To unpin an application or folder, right click on the app icon (or tap and hold the app icon). Then select **Unpin from taskbar**.

The second way to hide an application from the taskbar is by hiding the taskbar itself.

To do this:

- Right click an empty space on the taskbar (make sure you are not clicking any icon).

- Then select **Taskbar settings**.

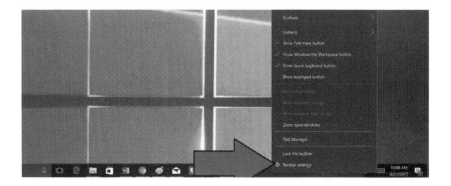

- Tap/Click the switch next to **Automatically hide the taskbar in desktop mode**. To also hide the taskbar in tablet mode, tap/click the switch next to **Automatically hide the taskbar in tablet mode**

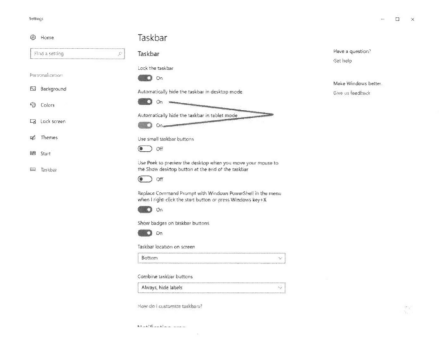

Taskbar

Taskbar

Lock the taskbar
On

Automatically hide the taskbar in desktop mode
On

Automatically hide the taskbar in tablet mode
On

Use small taskbar buttons
Off

Use Peek to preview the desktop when you move your mouse to
the Show desktop button at the end of the taskbar
Off

Replace Command Prompt with Windows PowerShell in the menu
when I right-click the start button or press Windows key+X
On

Show badges on taskbar buttons
On

Taskbar location on screen
Bottom

Combine taskbar buttons
Always, hide labels

How do I customize taskbars?

Home

Find a setting

Personalization

Background

Colors

Lock screen

Themes

Start

Taskbar

Have a question?
Get help

Make Windows better.
Give us feedback

To reveal the taskbar or the taskbar icons after hiding it, move your mouse pointer to the bottom of the screen where taskbar is usually located. This will let the taskbar icons show up. Note that the taskbar will disappear immediately you move away the mouse pointer.

To unhide the taskbar, follow the first two steps highlighted above and then tap the switch next to **Automatically hide the taskbar in desktop mode/ Automatically hide the taskbar in tablet mode**.

How to lock a taskbar

You may want lock taskbar so that it is fixed to a position. To do this, right click on an empty space on the taskbar and click on **Lock the taskbar.**

Note that if the **Lock the taskbar** feature is enabled, it will be impossible to drag the taskbar to any other part of the screen. However, you can still use the **Taskbar settings** options to move the taskbar to another position.

Changing taskbar color

Please note that you can also change the Start color and action center color by following the instructions provided below.

1. Right click while on the desktop and select **Personalize.**

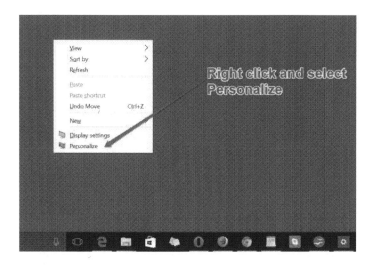

3. Alternatively, Press **Windows Key + I** and then click on **Personalization**.

4. Click on Colors. Tap the checkbox next to **Automatically pick an accent color from my background**. Then pick any color of your choice from the list of colors.

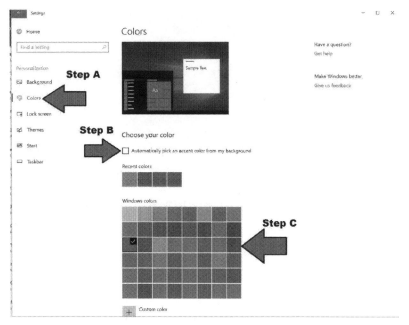

5. Tap the checkbox under **Show accent color on the following surfaces**.

 Please note that if you don't tap this checkbox, the color change will not reflect on the taskbar, start, action center, or title bars. Only the active icons/programs on the taskbar, notification area or the Start menu will assume the color.

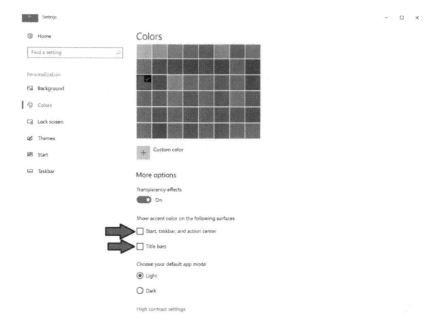

6. In addition, you can also make the Start, Taskbar, and Action center transparent by moving the slider under **Transparency effects**. Making the Start, Taskbar, and Action center transparent will allow their color to blend with the desktop color.

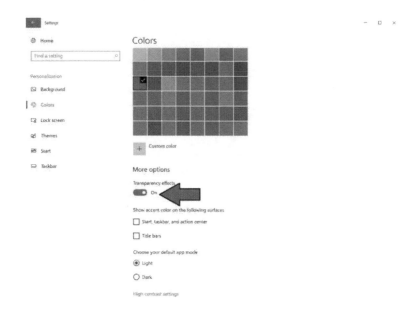

7. When you are done, close the settings by clicking on **X**.

Taskbar Problems and the Solution

Taskbar icons missing problem: What to do

You may sometime mistakenly hide your Taskbar and think that your it has disappeared. To fix this problem, follow the steps below:

- Move your cursor to the bottom of the screen, so that the taskbar shows up. Then right click on an empty space on the taskbar and select **Taskbar settings**.

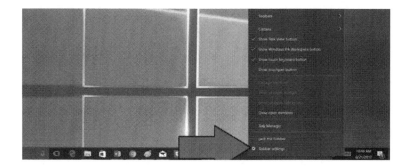

- Tap/Click the switch next to **Automatically hide the taskbar in desktop mode**. To also unhide the taskbar in tablet mode, tap/click the switch next to **Automatically hide the taskbar in tablet mode.**

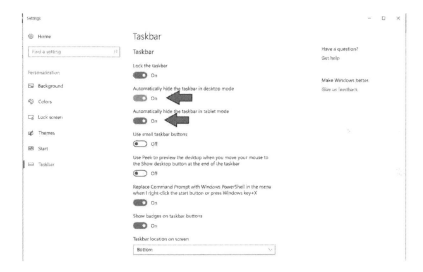

The problem of small taskbar and how to solve it

You may find out that the Taskbar icons are too small and you may want to increase their sizes. To do this, right click on an empty space on the taskbar and select **Taskbar settings**. Then tap the switch next to **Use small taskbar buttons**.

Action Center

Action center gives you a quick access to system notifications and settings.

Managing the Action Center Icons

You can rearrange the icons on the Action center to your taste. To do this, the steps to follow are given below:

1. Click on ⊞ > ⚙ **All settings > System > Notifications & actions.**
2. To move the Action Center icons to another place, tap and hold an icon and then drag it to a new location.

Tap and hold an
icon then drag it to
a new location

3. To add or remove an icon, tap **Add or remove quick actions.** Then use the switches to add or remove.

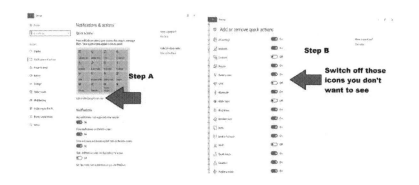

Step A

Step B

Switch off those
icons you don't
want to see

Handling Notifications on your Surface

Accessing notification center:

To see the notification center on your device, swipe in from the right edge of the screen.

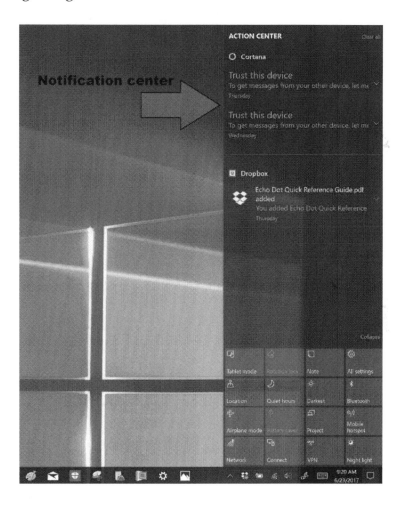

Disabling Notifications on Your Device

There are times that you don't want to see notifications at all or you don't want to see notification from certain apps. In this section of the guide, you will be learning how to do so.

To disable notification:

1. Swipe in from the right edge of the screen and click on **All Settings**
2. Click on **System**
3. Click on **Notifications & actions**.
4. To ensure that notification is turned completely off, ensure that these six options are turned off as shown below.

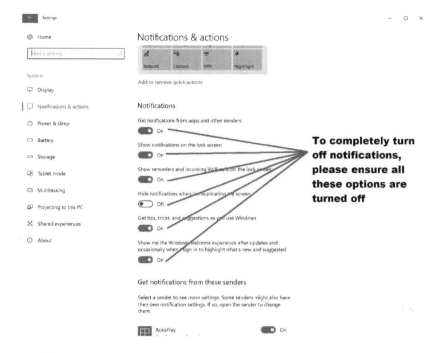

Disabling Notifications in Individual Apps

1. Repeat the first three steps mentioned above.

2. To turn off notifications from all apps, move the slider under **Get notifications from apps and other senders** to **Off** position. Please note that if you switch off this option, you will not be able to control notifications from individual apps.

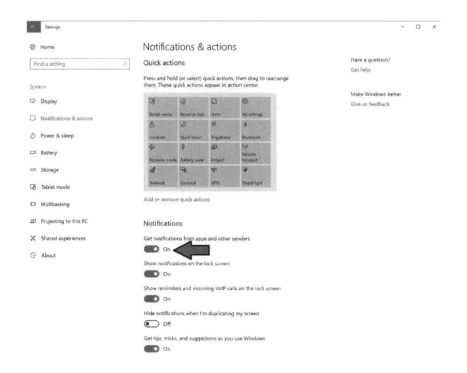

3. To manage notifications under individual apps, click on the
name of the individual app as shown below.

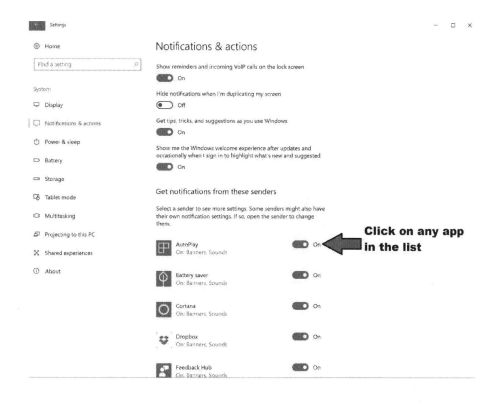

4. Then use the options under individual apps to customize each app. Please see the screenshot below.

You can use the fifth option on the screenshot below to control whether an app makes a notification sound.

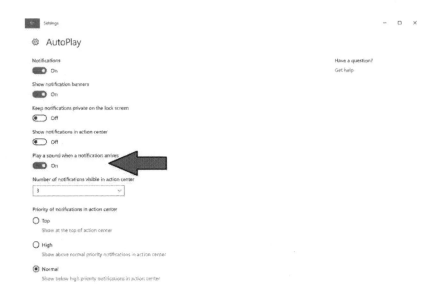

How to Turn off Notification While Making a Presentation on your Device

1. While in the notification settings screen, move the slider below **Hide notification when I am duplicating my screen** to **On** position.

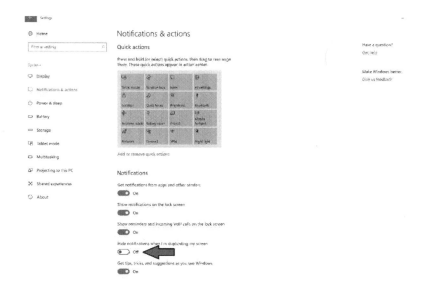

This should disable notifications while you are using your PC to make a presentation. This feature is particularly useful when you are in a meeting and talking on a subject.

Customizing Your Surface

You can get more done with your Surface by customizing it to match your preference. Please note that some of these customizations can be done when switching on your Surface for the first time. However, you may choose to customize your device at any time by following the instructions in the subsections below.

Managing the Language settings:

1. Swipe in from the right edge of the screen, Click **All settings** > **Time & language** > **Region & Language.**

2. To add a language, click on + **Add a language**.

3. To remove a language, click on the language you want to remove and select **Remove.**

Managing the Time and Date settings:

1. Swipe in from the right edge of the screen, and click **All settings** > **Time & language** > **Date and time**.

2. To set the time on your device manually or prevent your device from updating the time automatically; move the switch next to **Set time automatically** to **Off**, and then click on **Change** to edit the time and date as you desire.

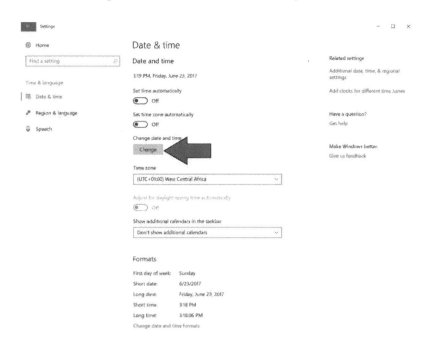

3. To manage the time zone settings, click on the dropdown menu below **Time zone** and select a time zone.

4. To change the format in which time is shown on your device, click on **Change date and time formats** (the last option on the screenshot below).

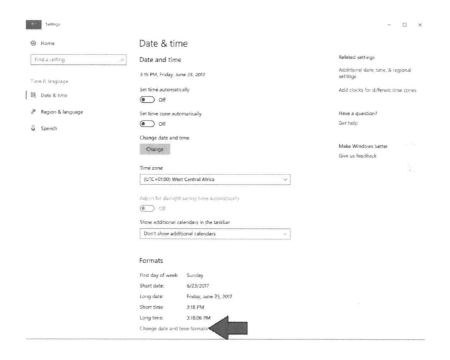

Tip: To quickly check the time in another country, select the search box in the Taskbar, enter **Clock**, and in the search results, select **Alarms & Clock**. Click on **World Clock**, and then click on **+** (located at the bottom of the screen). Type the name of a location in the search box that appears, and select a name from the list of proposed matches. See the red arrows in the screenshot below for more details.

To adjust your Surface's volume or switch to silent mode

1. Press the **Volume key** at the top of your Surface Pro to bring up the volume panel. Then adjust the volume of your device as you like. If you are using Surface Laptop, use the volume icon ◁») on the taskbar to adjust the volume.

Setting a screen lock image

You can set a screen lock image to the one of your choice. To do this:

1. Swipe in from the right edge of the screen, and Click **All settings > Personalization > Lock screen**.

2. Click on the dropdown menu next to **Background** and select **Picture**.

3. Then click on **Browse** and select an image (see the red arrow).

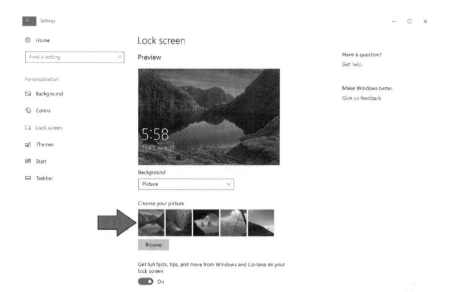

Tip: You can also choose **Slideshow** under the Background tab so that your Surface can rotate through all of the available lock screen scenes. In addition, you can also use the settings under **personalization/ lock screen** to choose which app shows information on your lock screen. To do this, click **All settings > Personalization > Lock screen**, and under **Choose an app to show detailed/quick status**, select the app(s).

Adjusting the brightness of the display

1. Swipe in from the right edge of the screen, and click **All settings > System > Display**. Then move the slider under the **Brightness level** as you like.

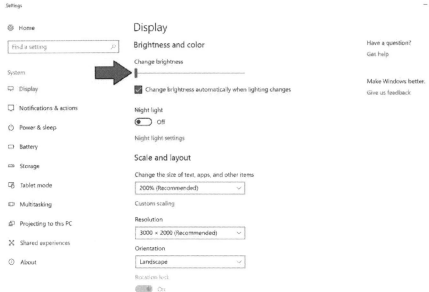

Home

Find a setting

System

Display

Notifications & actions

Power & sleep

Battery

Storage

Tablet mode

Multitasking

Projecting to this PC

Shared experiences

About

Display

Brightness and color

Change brightness

☑ Change brightness automatically when lighting changes

Night light
◉ Off
Night light settings

Scale and layout

Change the size of text, apps, and other items
200% (Recommended) ⌄
Custom scaling

Resolution
3000 × 2000 (Recommended) ⌄

Orientation
Landscape ⌄

Rotation lock
◉ On

Have a question?
Get help

Make Windows better.
Give us feedback

2. Alternatively, you may click on the search icon on the
 Taskbar and begin to type **Display** until you see **Change
 Display settings** at the top of the menu. Click it.

Hint: The brightness level of the display will affect how
quickly your Surface consumes battery power. I will advise
that you turn it reasonably low if you are very concerned
about saving the battery level on your Surface.

Understanding the Surface's keyboard

Both All New Microsoft Surface Pro and Microsoft Surface Laptop have keyboards. Note that Microsoft Surface Pro keyboard is sold separately. If you have Surface, you will probably be using it many times and it will be very cool to know how to operate it like a pro.

The first keyboard above is Microsoft Surface Pro Type Cover and the second keyboard above is Microsoft Surface Laptop keyboard.

The top row of surface keyboard contains special keys and functions keys.

Special key

Function key

Generally, when you press a key from top row, you will get a special key response. For example, if you press the ☀ / F1, you will be decreasing the brightness of your screen. But if you press Fn + front row key, e.g. Fn + ☀ / F1 you will get a function key response i.e. help in this case.

If you need to use function key a lot, you may lock the top row key to function key. To lock the function (Fn) keys, press the **Fn** key. To unlock, press the **Fn** key again.

Please note that a small light will appear on the **Fn** key when the top row keys are locked to the function mode.

In addition, you will be getting function keys responses when you press the front row keys while the **Fn** key is locked.

You can perform some functions on your Surface using the following special keys

Key icon	Function
Escape Key	cancel or abort operations
☀	Reduces the screen brightness
☀	Increases the screen brightness

▷‖	Plays or pauses audio or video file
◀×	Mute an audio
◁	Reduces audio volume
◀»	Increase audio volume
☼	Increase the keyboard backlight
PrtScn	Takes a screenshot. Note that to do this, you will need to press the Windows key ⊞ + **PrtScn**
Home	Allows you to go to the beginning of a line when using a Word Editor such as Microsoft Word.
End	Allows you to go to the end of a line when using a Word Editor such as Microsoft Word
PgUp	Moves up a page
PgDn	Move down a page
Del	Delete a text or words
☰	Opens the contextual menu. This is similar to what you will get when you right click.

Note: When I say you should press **Fn** + **F7** ☼, what I mean is that you should press and hold **Fn** key and then press **F7** ☼ key. You can also press these two keys simultaneously if you can.

Using Touchpad

Number	Function
1.	**Left touchpad button**: Use this button to select an item and perform other actions as you do with left-click on a mouse. **Tip**: To access left-click option without using the **Left touchpad button,** tap one finger anywhere on the touchpad.

2.	**Right touchpad button:** Use this button to open app commands or a context menu. You can also use it as you do with right-click on a mouse. **Tip**: To access right-click option without using the **Right touchpad button,** tap two fingers anywhere on the touchpad.
3.	**Touchpad:** Drag your finger on the touchpad to move the cursor. To scroll through a document, slide two fingers horizontally or vertically. **Tip**: To move an item on the desktop screen, double tap the item with a finger and then immediately (without removing your finger from the touchpad) drag your finger in any direction.

Tips:

While using the trackpad/touchpad, you may perform the following actions:

- Swipe three fingers up to view all opened apps.
- Swipe three fingers down to show the desktop.

- Swipe three fingers left or right to view all opened apps and switch among them. To flip through the opened apps, gently/slowly swipe three fingers left or right.

- Place two fingers on the touchpad and spread them apart to zoom in.

- Place two fingers on the touchpad and pinch them together to zoom out.

In addition, you can customize the mouse and touchpad settings on your device. To do this, select the search box in the taskbar, enter **Touchpad**, and in the search results, select **Touchpad settings**.

Using the Stylus Pen

One of the features that make using Surface very interesting is the Stylus/Surface pen. You can use Surface pen as you use normal writing pen. This pen will transform the way you interact with your device. In this section of the guide, I will be telling you how to use your Surface pen like a pro.

Downside: *Microsoft is now selling Surface Pen separately. It is no more included in the box.*

The Stylus pen uses **AAAA**-powered battery and it is designed to sleep whenever it is attached to the device or when it is not in use. These improvements extend the battery life of the **AAAA**-powered Pen so that you can use it for more than one calendar year.

Pair your Surface Pen with your Surface

To use your Surface Pen on your Surface you will need to pair the two together. To do this, follow the steps below:

1. Swipe in from the right edge of the screen and select **All Settings**
2. Select **Devices**
3. Select **Bluetooth & other devices** and make sure that the switch next to Bluetooth is On.

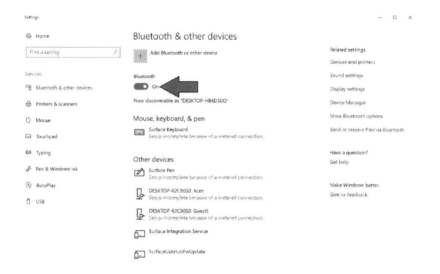

4. Hold down the top button of the pen for about seven seconds, until the light on the side of the pen glows.
5. When the pen appears in the list of Bluetooth devices, select it, and then click on **Pair**.

Special Notes

Please note that if you see your pen in the list of Bluetooth devices in step 3 above, select it, then click **Remove Device**. You are doing this to make sure that nothing affects your pairing process in step 4 and 5.

In addition, if your Surface fails to discover Surface Pen even though you have removed it, then try this: tap **Add Bluetooth or other device** and then tap **Bluetooth**; tap **Surface Pen** from the list that appears; and finally, tap **Done** after completing the setup. See the screenshot below.

Surface Pen Layout

Number	Function
1.	**Surface Pen Tip**: This tip allows you to write on the surface of your device. In addition, Microsoft sells Pen Tip Kit allowing you to choose your favorite tip. To learn how to adjust pen sensitivity, please go to page 72 and 73.
2.	**LED (Light-emitting diode)**: When the pen is in pairing mode, the LED glows.
3.	**Right-click button**: You can use this button just as you use the right click button on the

	track pad of the keyboard of your device. To use the Surface pen right-click feature, hold down the button as you tap the screen. This right-click feature works in many apps. Please note that unlike the top button on the Surface pen, the right-click button may not work when your Surface is asleep or when it is locked.
4.	**Top Button**: The top button transforms the way you use your Surface pen. With the top button, you can perform the following actions: • Click the top button to open Windows Ink Workspace. If enabled (see page 68), you can also use this feature even if your Surface is asleep. • Double-click the top button to use the Screen sketch option. The Screen sketch allows you to take a screenshot and write on it. • Click and hold the top button to open Sticky notes and jot down points.

Please note that Surface Pen has an inbuilt Bluetooth® technology, you may perform the actions mentioned above without moving your Pen closer to your Surface.

In addition, you may need to first pair your pen with your Surface (using Bluetooth) before you can use the top button. To pair your pen, please go to page 62.

Also, you can customize the top button of your Surface pen. To do this, please see below.

Customizing the Surface Pen top button

You can customize the top button to open the app you like. To do this:

1. Swipe in from the edge of the screen and select **All Settings**
2. Select **Devices**
3. Tap **Pen & Windows Ink**
4. Scroll down and choose an option you want to adjust.

Bluetooth & other devices

Printers & scanners

Mouse

Touchpad

Typing

Pen & Windows Ink

AutoPlay

USB

Learn about Windows Ink

Pen shortcuts

If your pen has a shortcut button, choose what to do when you press it. You might need to pair your pen via Bluetooth first.

Click once

Windows Ink Workspace

Home

Click once to open my Windows Ink Workspace notes even when the device is locked

On

Double-click

Windows Ink Workspace

Screen sketch

Press and hold (only supported on some pens)

Windows Ink Workspace

Sticky Notes

Using the dropdown boxes choose the apps to open with the top button

5. To be able to open the Windows Ink Workspace notes even when the device is locked, tap the switch next to **Click once to open the Windows Ink Workspace notes even when the device is locked.**

The Surface Pen, the Microsoft Edge and Other Pen Compatible Apps

You can use your Surface pen to write on the Microsoft Edge and also on apps that support pen input.

Generally, you can use your Surface pen anywhere you see the pen icons. This means that when an app has a pen icon then it should be compatible with Surface pen.

Surface pen tip works with Palm Block technology.

Using the Surface Pen and the handwriting panel

You can write something on the handwriting panel, and your Surface will automatically convert your words to text. To do this:

1. Click on the Keyboard icon on the lower part of the screen.

2. Click on 🎹 (located the right corner of the virtual

 keyboard) and then click on ✍️.

3. Start to write something on the screen. Surface will automatically convert your words to text.

Choosing right/left handedness

Choosing which hand you write with allows you to decide where menus appear on your Surface screen. To do this:

1. Swipe in from the right edge of the screen and select **All Settings**

2. Select **Devices**

3. Tap **Pen & Windows Ink**

4. Next to **Choose which hand you write with,** pick an option.

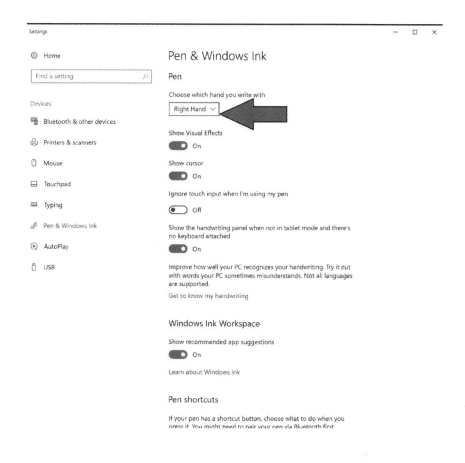

Changing the tips of your Surface Pen

If you have purchased the pen tip kit, you will probably need to remove the tip of your Surface pen at one time or the other. You can use the pen tip removal tool that accompanies your pen tip kit when you purchased it.

To change the pen tip:

1. Grasp the tip of the pen with the tip removal tool included with your pen tip kit and pull it straight out.
2. Insert the base of the new tip into the pen opening and push it in until it locks into place.

Using the Surface App

The Surface app allows you to use your device in a special way. With this app, you can control the pressure sensitivity of your Surface pen to suit your writing style. The app is free from the Windows Store.

Surface App Layout

The Surface app consists of the following options:

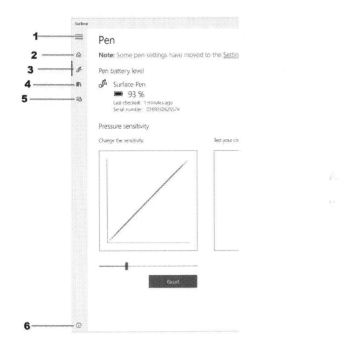

1. **Menu Button:** Click this to show the menu details or hide it.
2. **Home button:** Click on home button to gain access to the Surface app home screen
3. **Pen button:** Click on the pen icon to access the pressure sensitivity option and pen battery level.
4. **Help button:** Click on this to learn more about your Surface.
5. **Surface Info/Surface Registration Button**
6. **App Information button:** Click on this to get app information.

Airplane mode

In airplane mode, you can disable all wireless connections and network connection. This may be important in hospitals and airports. This feature also helps you save battery power.

To activate Airplane mode, swipe in from the right edge of the screen and click on the **Airplane or Flight mode** button.

Using The Special Features

Microsoft Surface Pro and Microsoft Surface Laptop came with special features that differentiate them from other devices. These special features are discussed below.

Microsoft Edge

Just like other Windows 10 devices, your Surface comes with a modern browser called Microsoft Edge. As far as Microsoft is concerned, Edge browser is the new browser of choice. It is much simpler and faster.

Please go to the section on **web browser** (see page 79) to learn more about this elegant browser.

Cortana

Another unique feature on your Surface is the Cortana. This is a trained virtual assistant that has been built to answer questions and interestingly, you probably don't need any technical training to use this feature. If you need any, it will be how to ask question that Cortana will understand. There is a section of this guide that has been written to show you how to manage Cortana like a pro and how to ask questions and give commands that Cortana will understand. This section can be found on page 202.

Windows Hello

Windows Hello on Surface is an iris-scanning bio-recognition software that allows you to sign in when you look at the frontal part of your Surface.

The iris-scanning bio-recognition software can be compared to fingerprint scanners present in other premium devices, but instead of using a finger to sign in, you will be using your face to sign in.

The camera on your device uses an infrared technology to identify your face or iris and can recognize you in a variety of lighting conditions. However, please note that this software may not be able to recognize your face in a very poor lighting condition.

To set up and use Windows Hello:

*If you don't already have one, please note that you may need to create a sign-in PIN before you can set-up Windows Hello. To set up a PIN, follow the steps 1-3 below and then Click **Add** under the **PIN** tab and follow the on-screen instructions. When you setup a new PIN, you will have the opportunity to choose how often your Surface requires sign-in.*

1. Swipe in from the right edge of the screen, and click **All settings.**

2. Click **Accounts**

3. Click **Sign-in options**

4. Click **Set-up** under Face Recognition.

5. Follow the on-screen instructions to complete the set-up process. If you wear glasses, you may need to remove it during the first setup. For best result, hold the screen of your Surface few inches away from your face.

6. If you wear glasses, click **Improve recognition** after the first setup, and then follow the on-screen instructions again.

7. To unlock your Surface while Windows Hello is enabled, press the power button. Hold the Surface up in front of your face, and wait for your Surface to recognize you. This may take some seconds.

Hint: *If Windows Hello doesn't work on time, please ensure that there is enough lighting condition where you are.*

Alternatively, you can use a PIN to sign in. To do this, swipe up on the lock screen and enter your sign-in PIN.

Furthermore, you can do more with Windows Hello, for example, you can purchase items from Windows store using Windows Hello, just click on the price button and follow the onscreen instructions.

Tip: If you are having problem setting up Windows Hello, check if your device settings are up-to-date. To see if there are updates, select the search box in the taskbar, enter **Update**, and in the search results, select **Check for update**. Then check if there are Windows updates.

Using the Web and the Apps

Microsoft Edge

Introduction

Gone are the days of Internet Explorer(IE) — the advent of Microsoft Edge has brought a tactical end to the famous IE. Adieu Internet Explorer! Adieu the most famous Web browser on earth!

In the view of the fact that Microsoft has chosen another favorite in the world of Web browsers, we must put the past behind us and get connected with the new born. Edge browser is the new born and we all have to know how to get started with it.

However, this does not mean that Internet Explorer is not on your Microsoft Surface Pro/Microsoft Surface Laptop. It is still part of the Windows 10 ecosystem, and since your device is running Windows 10, you can be sure that this browser is on your device. But you will not find it on the Taskbar nor the Start menu. You may need to use the search bar before you can find it.

As far as Microsoft is concerned, Edge browser is the new browser of choice. It is much simpler and faster. In addition, Edge browser makes it possible for you to write on Webpages and save it on OneNote or share it with your loved ones through emails. That is great, isn't it?

This comprehensive guide attempts to present Edge browser in a very clear and definitive manner so that both newbies and tech expert can get delighted reading it.

So, let's get started!

Opening the Edge Browser

The first thing you will need to do to access all the goodies that come with Microsoft Edge is to open it. This can be done by simply clicking on the **e** icon (a blue lowercase button) located on the taskbar.

Hint: There is a cool way to open the Edge browser from any File Explorer Windows's address bar. This is particularly faster if you are already doing something on the File Explorer and you quickly want to check for a webpage. Just type the Web address of the page you want to visit into the File Explorer window's address bar and hit **Enter** on the keyboard. For example, type wikipedia.com into a File Explorer window's address bar and hit **Enter** to open the Wikipedia page. See the screenshot below.

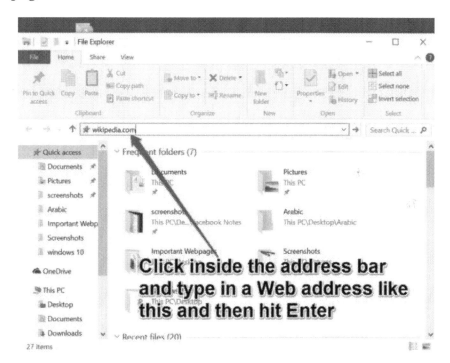

Get to know the Edge Browser Interface

The following screenshot will introduce you to the various features found on Edge browser:

1	Back: Click this icon to revisit the page you just visited.
2	Forward: Click this icon to return to the page you just left.
3	Refresh: Clicking this icon reloads a webpage.
4	Address bar: Clicking this bar allows you to enter the web address of a page. You may also type in search phrase into the address bar.
5	Reading View: Click this icon to get a page that is customized for reading. The reading view removes the ads and unnecessary information making it easier to read a webpage.
6	Add to Favorite or Reading List: Click this icon to add a webpage to your favorite or to add a webpage to your reading list so that you can read it later.

7	**Hub:** This tab gives you access to your reading list, favorites, histories, and downloaded files.
8	**Web note**: Clicking this icon enables you to annotate a webpage and save it on OneNote or share it with friends.
9	**Share**: Click on this icon to share a webpage with anybody.
10	**More Actions tab:** Click on this icon to access more options on Edge browser.
11	**Tabs you have set aside:** You can tap this icon to see those tabs you have set aside.
12	**Set these tabs aside:** Click on this icon to set all the tabs in the current window aside.
13.	**Close tab:** Click this to close a tab.
14	**Tab:** Tap this icon to navigate to a tab.
15	**Add new tab**: Click this to add another webpage.
16	**Show Tab Preview:** Tap this icon to see the tab preview.
17	**Minimize/Maximize Edge browser window**: Click this icon to reduce or enlarge the size of Edge Window.
18	**Restore down/Maximize tab:** Click this to restore down/enlarge a tab
19	**Close Edge browser window**: Click this icon to close the Edge browser and close all the opened tabs. Microsoft Edge browser will usually warn you when closing all tabs.

Hint: If you mistakenly click or tap a wrong button, don't panic, just keep holding your finger or mouse pointer on the wrong button and then stylishly move away your finger/mouse (just as if you are dragging the wrong icon) to stop the command from execution. Generally, command don't get executed until you release you finger or mouse pointer.

Customizing the Start-up Page

The startup page is the page that shows up when you open your Edge browser. When you open the Edge browser, what you will see can either be the start page, a blank page or a custom page. This all depends on the default setting or what you have commanded your browser to do. Fortunately, you can choose how this page is displayed.

You may choose to change the default startup page by following the steps below:

- Open the **More actions (...)** tab and click on **Settings**

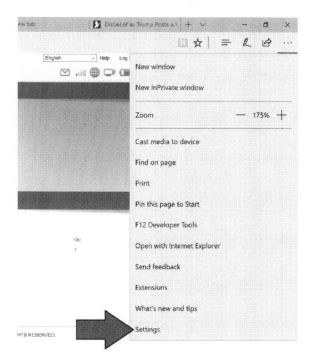

- Choose any of the following options under the **Open Microsoft Edge with** tab

 a) **Start page:** When you choose this option, Microsoft displayed news on your startup page. This news is powered by MSN.

 b) **New tab page:** If you want Edge browser not to display anything on your startup page then choose this option.

 c) **Previous pages:** When this option is chosen, your browser will load the pages you were viewing when last you closed it.

 d) **A specific page or pages:** This option is perfect for displaying your favorite webpages on the startup

page. You can choose to display one or more custom pages. For example, you can choose to display Wikipedia, WordPress and Google on your startup. To select a webpage of your choice, select **A specific page or pages** and then enter webpage of your own. Then tap the save icon when you are done. See the screenshot below.

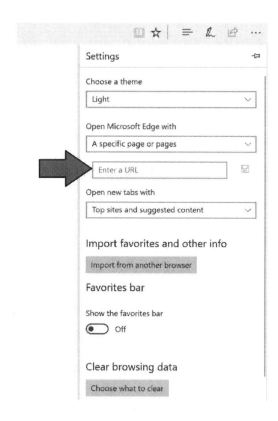

Hint: You can choose the webpage you wish to see first on the startup page by rearranging the custom webpages (specific pages) you have entered. To do this, navigate to the custom webpage settings page as shown above, and then drag webpages up and down in the list.

Using the Address/Search Bar

Every web browser must have an address bar and Edge browser also has one. This bar serves the function of URL address bar and search bar. By default, the searches done on this bar is executed by Bing. To learn how to change the search engine to Google, please go to page 105.

You choose whether to launch a webpage or search for a term based on what you type into the address bar.

For example, if you type **Windows Radar** into the address bar and press **Enter**, Bing search results for that phrase is displayed. On the other hand, if you type **windowsradar.com** and hit **Enter**, you will be taken to the website bearing the name.

Hint: To gain access to address bar straight away when using the Edge browser, Press **Ctrl + L** or **Alt + D.**

Furthermore, you don't have to type in the ".com" part of a URL, you can just type in the name (omit both the "www" and ".com" parts) and press **Ctrl + Enter**. For example, to go to Wikipedia, type in **Wikipedia** into the address bar and press **Ctrl + Enter.**

Edge browser makes website suggestions to you based on the sites you have recently visited. To choose any of these suggested sites, use the arrow key on the keyboard or the mouse to navigate the suggested sites and press **Enter** when you find the right one.

When you begin to type inside the address bar, Edge browser automatically makes suggestions beneath your typing. You can choose one of these suggestions to make things faster, provided that the suggestions truly read your mind.

In addition, you can choose to turn off the auto-suggestions feature by going to the Edge browser **Settings** and clicking on the **View advanced settings**. Then scroll down and click **Off** next to **Show search and site suggestions as I type**.

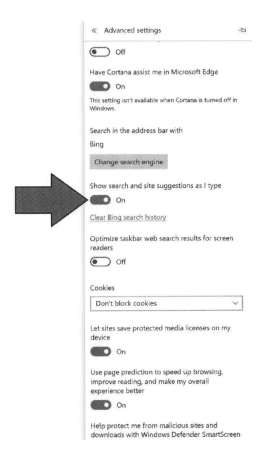

Controlling How You See the Webpages --
Using the Microsoft Edge Themes

Although not very robust, Microsoft Edge comes with themes. Basically, you can choose between two themes when using the browser. I will like to advise Microsoft to make more themes available.

The default theme that comes with Edge browser is light theme but you may change this to black by following these steps:

1. Open the **Settings** tab.

2. Click on the drop-down menu under **Choose a theme** and select **Dark**

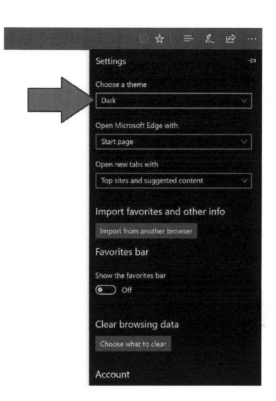

Navigating a Webpage- Scrolling Up/Down Smartly

When you open a long webpage, you will definitely have to scroll up and down. The traditional way to scroll a webpage is to use the mouse to move the slider, but there is a smarter way to do this. When next you want to scroll up, press **Page Up** or **Page Down** on the keyboard to scroll up or down respectively. In addition, you can use the arrow keys to scroll up/down. Pressing **Shift + Space bar** will also scroll up a webpage.

Zooming a Webpage in Edge Browser

To zoom a webpage in Microsoft Edge, press **Ctrl** and **+** key to zoom in and press **Ctrl** and **-** key to zoom out. Alternatively, open the **More actions (...)** tab and click on plus or minus sign next **Zoom.**

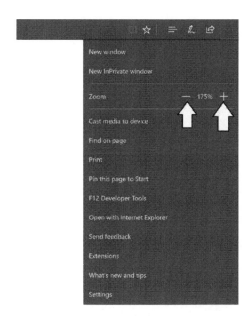

Using tabs on Edge browser

You can open many tabs at once on Edge browser. You can navigate different opened webpages by clicking the tabs above the window of these webpages. Please see the screenshot under **Get to know the Edge Browser Interface** (see page 82) to have a pictorial view of Edge browser tabs.

You can use the following keyboard shortcuts to manage tabs:

- **Ctrl + T**: Open a new tab

- **Ctrl + W**: Close a tab

- **Ctrl + Tab:** switch from one tab to the next

- **Ctrl + K**: Open a new duplicate tab of the tab you are presently viewing

- In addition, you can move straight to a tab by pressing **Ctrl** and the number of the tab. For example, to move to the fourth tab press **Ctrl + 4**

- To open a link in a separate tab, press **Ctrl** and that link.

What of the Home Button?

You might have asked yourself at one time or the other the location of Home button when using the Edge browser. Fortunately for the Home button fans, there is a Home button in the Microsoft Edge. However, you will need to tell the browser that you want to see it before it can be displayed to you.

To show the Home button in your browser:

1. Click on the **More actions (...)** tab

2. Click on **Settings**

3. Click on the **View Advanced settings**

4. Next to **Show the home button,** select **On**

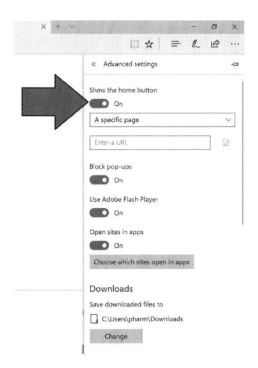

5. Select **A specific webpage** from the dropdown menu and type a webpage address in the space provided and click **Save** ⊟ . If you type in a webpage address, the Edge browser will open this webpage whenever you click the home button.

Favorites (Bookmarks)

With several billions of webpages in the internet world, you just have to select your favorites. Just like any other modern day browsers, Microsoft Edge gives you the opportunity to select a favorite or to bookmark a page. This makes it easier to visit the website or webpage in the future.

To add a website to favorites:

1. Open the website you want to bookmark

2. Press **Ctrl + D.** Alternatively, you may click on the favorite icon on the address bar. See the screenshot below:

3. Tap in the **Name** you want.

4. Click **Add.**

Accessing Your Favorites

After you have added a webpage to your Favorites list, you will need to access this list sooner or later. To access the Favorites list, press **Ctrl + I.** Alternatively, you may click the **Hub** icon and then click on Favorites icon .

Hub icon

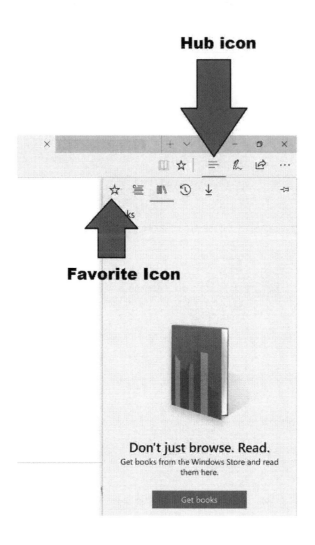

Favorite Icon

Don't just browse. Read.

Get books from the Windows Store and read them here.

Get books

What about the Favorite bar?

The favorite bar is the favorite panel beneath the address bar. This bar is not there by default, you will need to activate it yourself if you want to see it. Displaying the favorite tab allows you to access your most used webpages with just a single click.

- There are two ways to make the Favorites bar appear on your browser. The first and faster way is to click **Ctrl** + **Shift** + **B.** To remove the Favorites tab, press this command again. The second way is to go to your Edge browser **Settings** and select **On** under **Show the favorites tab.**

- Click the **Hub** icon and then click on Favorites icon .

- Drag and drop favorite website into the Favorite Bar folder.

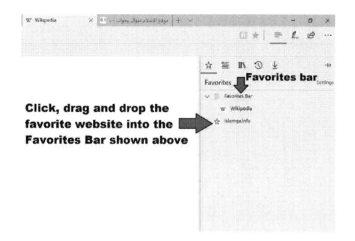

Hint: *You can rearrange how the webpages appear on your Favorite Bar. To do this, click and drag a webpage on the favorite bar to left or right.*

Importing your bookmarks from other browsers

When you start using the Edge browser, you will like to import your bookmarks from other browsers. To import your bookmarks to Edge browser:

1. Open the **More actions (...)** tab and click on **Settings**

2. Click on **Import from another browser.**

3. Select browsers from the list and click on **Import.**

Managing the Reading List

Webpages contain a lot of information and you will probably need to schedule some webpages for a later reading. Microsoft Edge reading list is a great way to do this. When you find an interesting information online and you don't have the time to read it, you can save it for later reading by keeping it in your reading list.

The reading list is one of the features under the **Hub** tab.

The fastest way to access the reading list is by pressing **Ctrl + G.** Alternatively, a slower way will be to click on the **Hub** icon and then click the reading list icon.

To add a webpage to the reading list, open the webpage and click on the star icon as though you are about to add a Favorite. In the dialog box that appears, select **Reading list** tab. Edit the name, if you like, and click on **Add.**

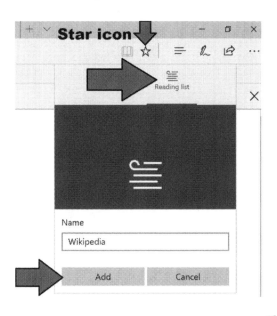

Alternatively, you may press **Ctrl + D** and select **Reading list** and then select **Add.**

Downside: It appears that Reading list in Edge browser is not very robust as one would have loved. Although Microsoft Edge saves the web-address, it appears that it does not actually store the webpages on your PC so that you can read them offline later. This mean that you will still need internet connection to read the webpages in your reading list.

Understanding the Edge Browser Reading View

The Edge browser reading view allows you to read a webpage in an optimized way. The reading view is customized for better reading. It gives you access to just text and images on a webpage eliminating adds and other unnecessary information on a webpage.

To activate the reading view on a webpage, press **Ctrl + Shift + R.** Alternatively, you can click on the reader button on the address bar. To exit the reading view, click the reading view button again or press **Ctrl + Shift + R**

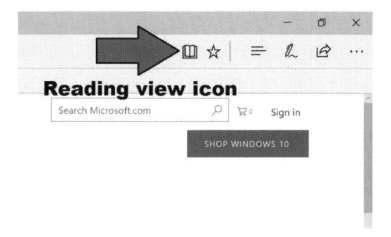

Note: Not all webpages are supported by the reading view; the reading view icon will appear bold if the webpage you are viewing is supported.

Customizing the reading view

You can make some tweaks to reading view by going to the settings. To customize the reading view, click on reading view icon (see the screenshot above). Then click on Font/Theme icon and select an option:

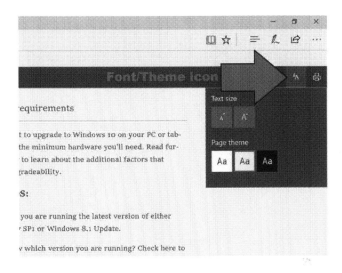

Changing the Search Engine

The default search engine on Microsoft Edge is Bing. Many people will love to change this to Google.

You can change the Microsoft Edge Search Engine (Bing) to Google by following the steps highlighted below:

1. Click the menu icon (**...**) and click on **Settings**

2. Click **View advanced settings**.

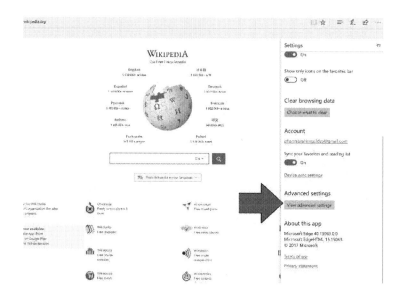

3. Click on **Change Search engine** and select Google if it is present in the list. If not, it is because Edge browser has not discovered it. For Edge browser to discover Google, go to *google.com* using the Edge browser, and then go back to **Change Search Engine.** After you have clicked on Google, click on **Set as default** to make Google your default search engine on Microsoft Edge.

Setting a Tab Aside

Edge Browser gives you the opportunity to set some tabs aside to better control your working space.

To set a tab aside:

1. Open all the tabs you want to set aside.

2. Tap **Set these tabs aside** icon.

Set these tabs aside icon

3. To restore all the tabs you have set aside, tap the **Tabs you have set aside** icon. Then tap **Restore tabs.**

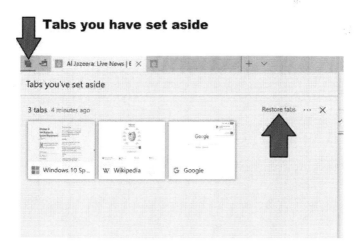

Tabs you have set aside

Tip: To add all the tabs you have set aside to favorite list, just click on the three dots icon (...) next to **Restore tabs** and then select **Add tabs to favorites.**

Managing the History List

Edge browser collects the history of the webpages you visit and stores it.

There are many ways you can manage Microsoft Edge browsing history, but some ways are smarter than others.
In this section of the guide, I will tell you a smart way to quickly manage your browsing history.
You can manage your Edge history smartly with these three keyboard shortcuts:

1. Use **Ctrl + H** to access browsing history from any tab in Microsoft Edge Browser. By just pressing these two keys, you will have the browsing history opened before you.

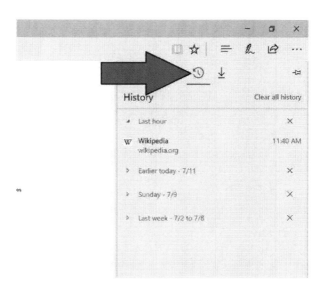

2. Use **Ctrl + J** to access Edge browser download history. Press these two keys and gain access to all your past downloads.

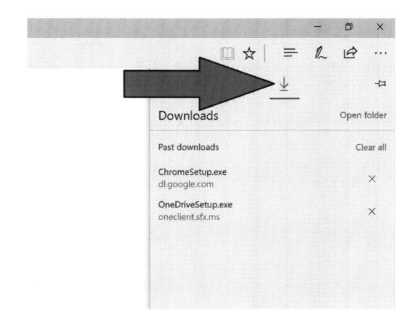

3. Use **Ctrl + Shift + Delete** to access **Clear browsing data** page and clear your browsing history.

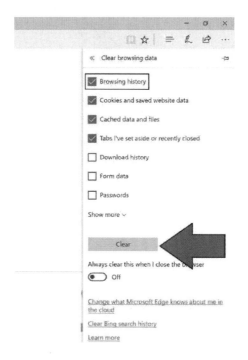

Using Cortana on Edge Browser

Cortana is probably the most famous feature on Windows 10 and you can be sure that it is also integrated with Microsoft Edge.

Cortana is a voice-controlled personal assistant on Windows 10. With some text command, you can activate this feature.

While using your Edge browser, you can use Cortana in the following ways:

- **Address bar search**: When you type in some specific phrases into the address bar on the Edge browser, you can put Cortana to work. For example, to check the weather of New York, type in **Weather 10024.** This should give you the New York weather information even before you press **Enter** key.

- **More info about a phrase**: If you are reading an article and you encounter a word or phrase that is difficult, you can quickly ask Cortana. Just select the text and right click on it. Then choose **Ask Cortana.** See the red arrow.

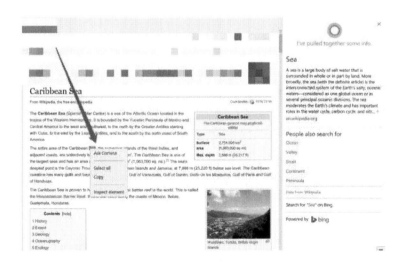

Using the Web Note

Microsoft is very proud of the fact that Edge browser allows you to annotate a webpage. To the best of my knowledge, as at the time of writing this guide, it is the only modern day browser that gives you that opportunity.

To annotate a webpage:

- Open the webpage and click on the markup button in the top-right corner of Edge browser.

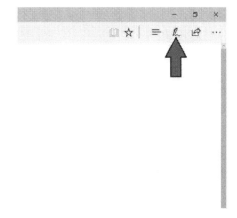

- Use the following tools to get a beautiful annotation:

1. **Pen:** Use this just like you will use your pen. When you click the pen icon twice, you are given the option of choosing the color and the size/pen thickness. You can use the Surface pen (if you have one) to make annotations as you like.

2. **Highlighter:** Think of this as a marker you use on paper. You can use the highlighter button to highlight a text to pay a special attention to it. Just like pen tool, you can also select the color or size of the highlighter by clicking the highlighter icon twice.

3. **Eraser**: Every writer needs an eraser, and you surely also need one. Edge browser gives you the opportunity to erase a markup in case you make a mistake. You can erase all your annotations by clicking eraser icon twice and selecting **Erase all ink**.

4. **Typed notes:** This looks like a comment box. When you click this icon and then click any part of a webpage, a little box appears to let you add special note to the webpage. You can move the typed note by dragging its handle. You can also minimize a typed note by clicking on the handle just once. To delete a typed note, click on the **Delete icon** 🗑 . The typed note box automatically

increases in size to accommodate new notes as you type in more words.

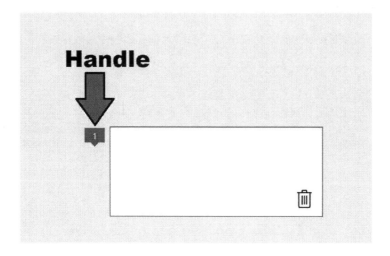

5. **Clip:** This is akin to what we have in other image editors. You can use this tool to copy a part of a webpage. When you click this icon, you will be asked to drag to copy a region of a webpage. When you drag the rectangular box and release it, this webpage is copied to your clipboard. You can then paste it to Microsoft Word or other similar programs by pressing **Ctrl + V.**

6. **Pan**: This tool allows you to move the webpage in order to see other parts of the webpage. To pan, just select this tool and then click, hold and drag in various directions.

7. **Save Web Note:** Tap this to save your web note.

8. **Share Web Note:** Tap this icon to share your web note.

9. **Exit:** Click this to exit the web note.

Export/Saving a Web Note

After spending some time annotating a webpage, you will need to save it to avoid losing your work. When you click the **Save icon**, you will have the chance to save your work to the following places:

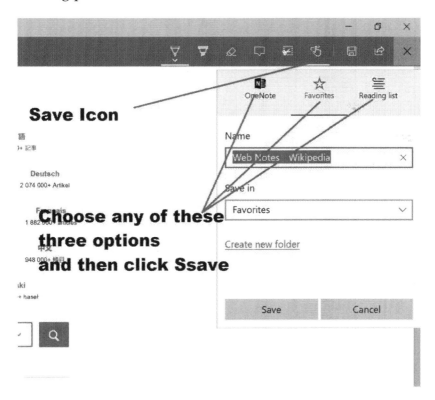

- **OneNote**: You can choose this option to have your annotation stored as a note in OneNote.

- **Favorites:** You can choose to save your markup as a favorite. You can also save the web note in a new favorite folder by clicking the **Create new Folder.** In addition, you can type a name for your annotated webpage before saving it in favorites.

- **Reading List:** Similar to Favorites, you can also save the markup as one of the items on your reading list. You may type a name for your annotated webpage before saving it in the reading list.

Notes:

- When a markup is saved to Favorite or Reading List, you can choose to hide annotation when viewing it by clicking on **Hide.**

- Although you have the opportunity to edit the web note when you save it in reading list or favorites, it appears that you will need to save another copy of this web note after you are done editing. Edge browser will not replace your web note with the new edited version, but will save the newly edited one as another version.

Sharing Your Web Note with Friends

To share your web note with friends or email it to someone, click on the **Share** button located beside the save button. Then choose a social media from the sharing options that appear.

Closing the Web Note

When you are done with making a web note, click on **Exit icon**

Printing Web Pages on Microsoft Edge

Printing on Microsoft Edge is quite fantastic. I love the fact that Edge browser neatly fits a webpage within the print page. You can initiate the printing process by pressing **Ctrl + P.**

Alternatively, you can click on **More actions** (...) tab and select **Print.**

You can use these various options on the print window to customize what comes out of your printer. These Options include:

- **Orientation**: This option allows you to choose between portrait and landscape.

- **Pages:** Choose between printing the current page or just enter the range of pages to print. You can also print all pages by selecting **All.**

- **Scale**: Use this option to tell the printer whether to shrink the webpages to fit or choose from scaling options. Choosing a lower scaling option like 50% allows you to save paper because more words will be printed on a page. However, the fonts may be too small if you choose a small scaling option.

- **Margins**: Use this option to tell your printer which margin to leave on the paper. You can choose between normal, narrow, moderate, or wide. Choosing a narrow margin will ensure that you print more words per page and thereby save paper.

- **Headers and footers**: Use this option to tell your printer whether to include URL of the webpage and the name of the webpage in the header and the footer.

- **More settings:** This gives you access to **paper size and quality** and **page layout.**

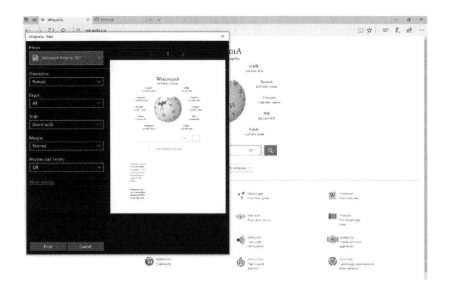

It is important to mention that some webpages give you the opportunity to print their web information by clicking on the **Print icon** located on their webpages. When you have a situation like this, I will advise that you print the webpage using the Print icon located on the webpage. This is because a website print feature usually eliminates ads and other unnecessary information from a print page making sure that the printout will not be chopped off or distorted.

Edge InPrivate Browsing

There are times when you will not want your browser to save any information about your visit to a webpage. For instance, if you don't want a website to save cookies on your device or you don't want your child to know you are browsing about favorite gifts to buy for them.

In addition, InPrivate mode browsing allows for multiple sessions, for example, you may access your Yahoo mail account (or another web account) on a normal window and use the secret mode tab to open the Yahoo mail account of that of your friend or family member without logging out of your own account. Pages viewed in secret mode are not listed in your browser history or search history, and leave no traces (such as cookies) on your device.

To activate InPrivate browsing, click the **More actions** (...) button and select New InPrivate window.

How to Pin a Menu in the Edge Browser

When you access the Microsoft Edge settings, you will realize that it normally covers a sizable part of a webpage, to eliminate this constraint and make sure that the settings tab is easily accessible, I will advise that you pin the settings menu to the browser. To do this, open the browser's settings tab and then click on the pin icon located on the settings pane.

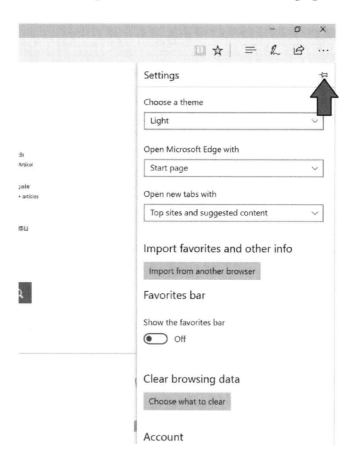

Please note that you can also pin other items like the reading list and favorites to the Edge browser. Just click on the pin icon as described above. To remove the pin feature, click on the **X** icon.

More on Edge Browser Settings

Many options under Edge Settings have already been discussed but there are some other ones that I will like to mention.

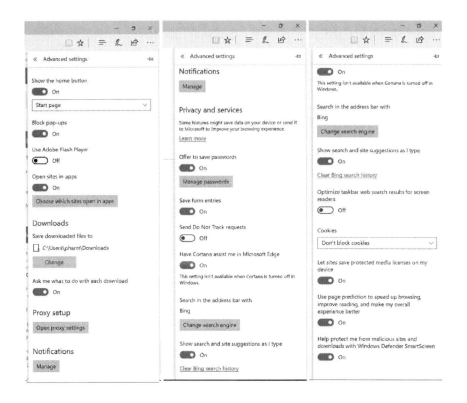

1. **Block pop-ups:** This option allows you to block websites from opening a pop-up window.

2. **Use Adobe Flash Player:** Enabling this option makes it possible to play the flash contents of many websites automatically.

3. **Open sites in apps:** Some websites can be opened by an app and you can use the option to manage the sites. To do this, make sure the option is enabled and then click on **Choose which sites open in apps.**

4. **Download:** To change where to save your downloads, click on **Change** and then choose a folder.

5. **Proxy Setup:** Use this option to manage internet proxy settings. You may not bother with this as the automatic settings might just be enough.

6. **Notifications:** Use this option to manage websites that will show you notifications.

7. **Offer to save passwords**: You probably have tens of different passwords. You can use this Edge feature to allow the browser to offer to save your password whenever you enter a password or login information in a new website. In addition, click on **Manage passwords** to make changes to your saved passwords.

8. **Save form entries:** Use this option to enable Microsoft Edge to save your form entries whenever you fill in information into an online form.

9. **Do not send track request**: Use this option to discourage websites from tracking you.

10. **Have Cortana assist me in Microsoft Edge**: Use this option to enable Cortana to work with Edge browser.

11. **Search in the address bar with**: Please refer to page 105 to learn more.

12. **Show search and site suggestions as I type**: Use this option to allow Edge browser to show search suggestions when searching for an information.

13. **Optimize taskbar web search results for screen readers:** When this option is enabled, your Edge browser should optimize Taskbar web search results based on the screen readers.

14. **Cookies:** Use this option to control cookies settings.

15. **Let sites save protected media licenses on my device:** Use this option to allow website to save licensed media materials on your Surface.

16. **Use page prediction to speed up browsing, improve reading, and make my overall experience better:** Edge browser will speed up your browsing experience if this option is enabled.

17. **Help protect me from malicious sites and downloads with Window Defender SmartScreen:** SmartScreen filter is a feature that protects you from phishing

websites and malicious software. I will advise that you always keep this feature **On**.

More on the More actions (...) tab

Many options under the More actions (the three dots icon) tab have already been discussed, but I will like to explain the remaining items that have not been discussed.

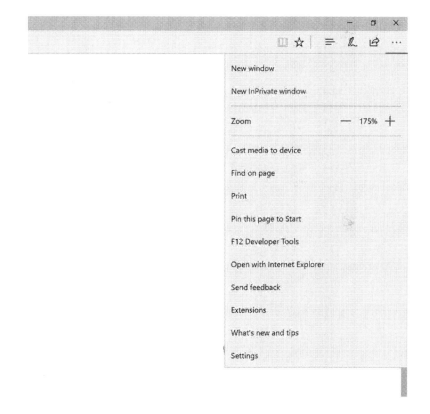

1. **Zoom**: Use this option to zoom in or zoom out a webpage.

2. **Cast media to device**: Use this option to cast what you are viewing on Edge browser to another screen.

3. **Find on page:** Use this option to search for a word or a phrase on a webpage.

4. **Pin this page to Start:** Use this option to pin a webpage to the Start.

5. **F12 Developer Tools:** Use this option to access Microsoft Edge developer tools. This is useful for programmers.

6. **Open with Internet Explorer:** You can open a webpage in Internet explorer by clicking this option.

7. **Send feedback:** Use this option to report an issue to Microsoft.

8. **Extensions:** Use this option to access Edge browser extensions.

9. **What's new and tips:** Use this option to learn more about Edge browser.

What about Microsoft Edge Extensions

Extensions open a new world for many internet users. It allows you to use your Edge browser in a special way. To access extension, click the More actions (...) button and select **Extension**.

How to Save a Webpage for Offline Use in Microsoft Edge

Unfortunately, the usual **Ctrl + S** is not working on Edge browser. In fact, if you save a webpage in reading list, you will still need an internet access to read it. This means that there is no direct way to save a web page for offline reading in Edge browser.

Fortunately, there is a way round this problem. To save a webpage for offline reading:

1. Click the Web Note icon.

2. Click Save icon.

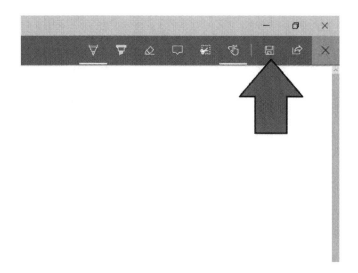

3. Choose one of Favorites, Reading list or OneNote and then click on **Save.**

How to download a file in Edge browser

1. Open the webpage.

2. Locate and click on the download link.

3. Click **Save.**

4. Wait for the download to finish and click on **Open.**

Please note that if you are downloading a pdf document, it will automatically open with the Edge browser pdf reader.

You can pause a download by clicking on **Pause** while the file is still downloading. Please note that to use this option, the file will still need to be downloading. If the file has already been downloaded completely, the **Pause** button will not be available.

What about the Edge Browser PDF Reader.

Just like many modern-day web browsers, Microsoft Edge has an inbuilt PDF Reader. To use the Edge PDF Reader, right click on the document that you want to read and select **Open with.** Then select **Microsoft Edge**.

The Shortcut keys in the Edge browser

Many keyboard shortcuts have already been mentioned in this guide, but I will still mention new ones.

Press **Ctrl** + **T** to open a new tab.

Press **Ctrl** + **H** to access browsing history in Edge browser.

Press **Ctrl** + **J** to access Microsoft Edge download history.

Press **Ctrl** + **P** to print a page.

Press **Ctrl** + **N** to open a new Window.

Press **Ctrl** + **F** to find any word or phrase on a webpage.

Press **Ctrl** + **D** to add a page to Favorite/Reading list.

Press **Ctrl** + **Shift** + **Delete** to access Clear browsing data page.

Troubleshooting Edge Browser

Being an app, Edge browser may sometime refuse to work properly or it may be hanging. If any of these happens, just close the browser and open it again. If the browser refuses to close then Press **Ctrl** + **Alt** + **Delete** and choose **Task Manager** from the dialog box that appears. Then right click on **Microsoft Edge** and choose **End task.**

Conclusion

Edge Browser is a new comer to the world of web browsers and there are still many things that Microsoft needs to improve. That being said, I strongly believe that this guide will help you with this browser so that you can use it like a pro.

Mozilla Firefox

Mozilla Firefox is one of the most used browsers in the world, and you will probably love to know how to get started with this browser on your Surface.

In this section of the guide, you will be learning the various tips and tweaks on Mozilla Firefox.

So let's get started!

Please note that Mozilla Firefox is not preinstalled on your Surface, and to use it, you will need to download and install it.

Where can I download Mozilla Firefox?

The best place to download Firefox for your Surface is Firefox Website. It is important you download it from their website because you will have the opportunity of downloading the most recent version of Firefox.

You can follow this link to download Firefox right now!

How to Import your bookmarks from other browser to Mozilla Firefox

When you start using Firefox, one of the first things you will want to do is to import you bookmarks from other browsers. To do this, press **Ctrl + Shift + B** to open the bookmark tab and the click on **Import and Backup.** Then select **Import data from another browser.**

Then choose a browser

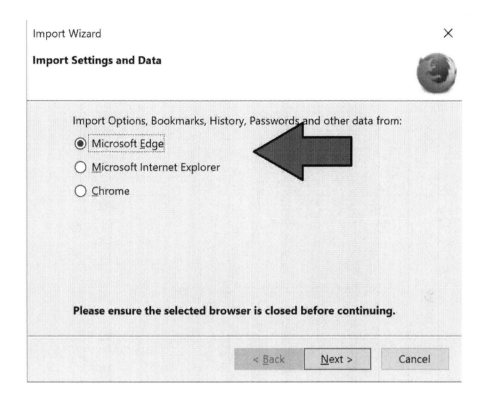

Select what to import and choose **Next.**

Then click on **Finish** after the successful completion.

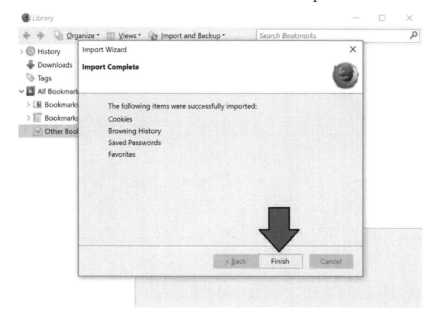

To check the imported data, navigate to the bookmark tab by clicking on the bookmark icon, click **Bookmarks Toolbar** and the select an option. See the screenshot below.

How to Make Firefox Your Default Browser

The default browser on your device is Microsoft Edge and you may want to change this to Mozilla Firefox. To make Firefox your default browser, follow the instructions below:

1. Open the Firefox browser and click on **menu icon** and then click on **Option.**

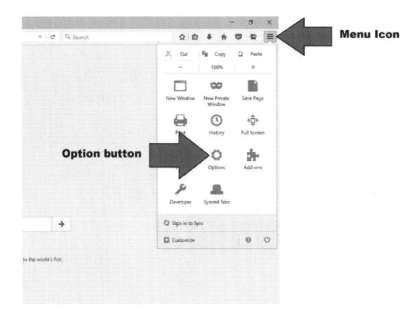

2. Under the **General** tab, click on **Make Default**. Please note that this option may not be available if Firefox is already your default browser.

3. You will then be taken to the app selection page, click on the drop-down menu and select **Mozilla Firefox**.

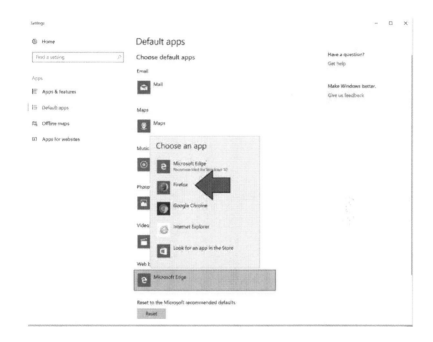

Please note that you may also change your default browser by going directly to the **Default apps** under **Settings.** To locate the **Default apps,** open the **Settings** tab, click on **Apps.** Then click on **Default apps**.

Keyboard Shortcuts to Use on Mozilla Firefox

There are many keyboard shortcuts that you can use on Mozilla Firefox, and some of the important ones are mentioned below:

1. Use **Ctrl + H** to access browsing history from any tab in Mozilla Firefox. By just pressing these two keyboards shortcut, you will have the browsing history opened before you.

2. Use **Ctrl + J** to access Mozilla Firefox download history.

3. Use **Ctrl + Shift + Delete** to access Clear browsing data page.

4. Use **Ctrl + N** to open a new Window.

5. Use **Ctrl + T** to open a new tab.

6. Use **Ctrl + Shift + A** to open the Add-on tab.

7. Use **Ctrl + F** to find any word or phrase on a webpage.

8. Use **Ctrl + Shift + B** to open the bookmark tab.

9. Use **Ctrl + D** to add a page to Favorite list.

10. Press **Alt** to open menu bar.

11. Use **Ctrl + P** to print a page.

12. Use **Ctrl + S** to save a page for offline use.

13. Use **Ctrl + O** to open Firefox download folder.

How to Customize Mozilla Firefox

You may want to customize the look of Firefox on your device. To do this, open the Firefox browser, click on the menu icon and then click on **Customize**.

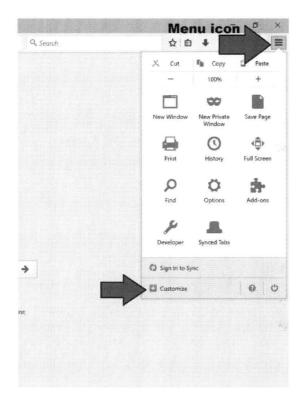

Then drag any of the icons to any location you want. You may also perform any of the following:

Use **Show/Hide Toolbar** to display or hide the toolbar;

You can reset your customization to default settings by clicking in the **Restore Defaults** icon;

You can also use the **Title Bar** option to display Firefox title.

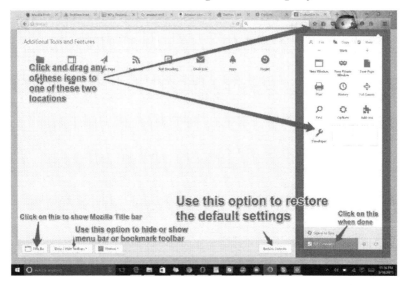

How to customize/change Mozilla Firefox themes

You may use the theme option to change Mozilla Firefox skin. To do this, open the Firefox Menu tab and click on **Customize** as shown in the preceding section. Then click **Themes,** then select a theme from the list as shown below.

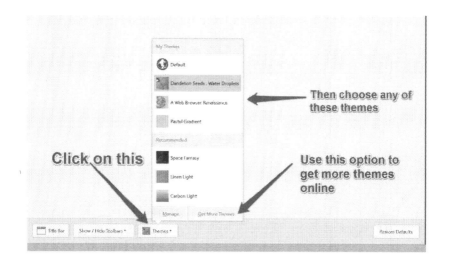

Click on this

Then choose any of these themes

Use this option to get more themes online

Using the Firefox Settings Options

The **Options** tab under the menu tab can be used to perform many actions. If you are just using the Mozilla Firefox for the first time, the default settings should be OK for you. However, you may still want to check the Privacy tab and the Security tab to see if everything is in the right condition. See the screenshot below.

You may also check all other options in order to be sure that everything is Ok.

Please note that you can access the Firefox

Settings **Options** by following the instructions under **How to Make Firefox Your Default Browser** (see page 139).

How use Microsoft store app

Your Surface functionality can be extended by installing different kinds of applications. Microsoft store provides you with an easy access to shop for free apps & paid apps, books, services etc.

 ➢ **To access the store app**

1. Select the search box in the Taskbar, enter **Store**, and in the search results, select **Store**.

2. To quickly search for a product while viewing an item, tap on the search icon (**magnifying glass icon**) located at the upper right corner of the screen and type whatever you want to search for. You can also choose a product from the categories.

3. To buy the product, tap the price. If the item offers a free trial, tap **Free trial** to try the item for free for a limited time. If the item is free, tap **Free/Install/Get**.

Note: You may be prompted to enter your Microsoft account information when using this shopping app for the first time.

 ➢ **Downloading and Installing Apps**

The Microsoft store gives you the opportunity to download apps to your device. To do this:

1. Select the search box in the Taskbar, enter **Store**, and in the search results, select **Store**.

2. Using the search icon, search for the apps you want to download. You may use the **dropdown box** at the top of the top of the screen to customize your search.

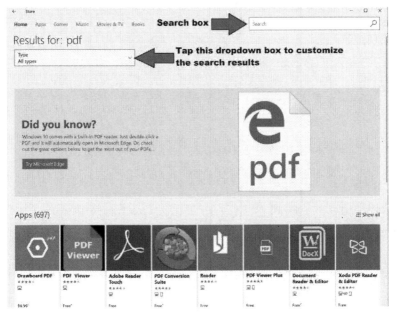

3. When you have seen the app you are looking for, tap on it to go to the details page.

4. When you are on the details page, tap on **Free/Install/Get**, or if it is a paid app, tap on the button bearing the price.

5. You can pause an ongoing download by taping on ||, to resume a download, tap ↻.

6. When the app has finished downloading, tap on **Open/Launch**.

7. If prompted to agree to terms of service (TOS), tap **Agree** if you agree with the TOS and then follow the onscreen instructions to complete the installation process.

➢ **To uninstall an application**

Click on the Windows icon on the Taskbar and then look for the app you want to uninstall. Right-click or long tap on the application you want to uninstall and then select **Uninstall.** Please note that you may not be able to uninstall those apps that came with your Surface.

➢ **Write a review for an app**

You can share your opinion on an app with other Store users.
To do this:

1. Open the app store and navigate to the app, scroll down
and tap Rate and review.

2. Rate the app, and write your review.

➢ **Getting more from the Store app**

You can get more options when using Store app by clicking on

and choosing an option.

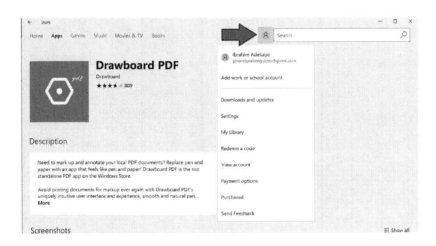

Updating your Apps

Depending on your settings, an installed app should automatically update when the developer releases a new software version for the app. However, if the app requires new permissions, you may need to visit Microsoft Store to manually update the app. To manually update an app:

- From the home scree, tap on **Store**.

- Click on and then tap **Downloads and updates**.
- Tap **Get Updates,** located at the top right corner of the screen.

Tip: To see the number of apps currently downloading or updating, check if there is any icon like the one shown below.

The number usually signifies the number of apps currently download or updating.

Using other apps on your Surface

You can access any preinstalled app on your Surface by
tapping or clicking its icon. You may be required to accept
terms of service when using an app for the first time. Use the
onscreen icons to perform different tasks in an app. To access
more features on a particular app, tap ☰ or ... (if available).

Communication

MAIL APP

Introduction

All New Microsoft Surface Pro and Microsoft Surface Laptop come preloaded with Mail app for sending and receiving emails, and one of the things you will need to do when you start using your device is to set up an email account.

Your device Mail app has a support for IMAP and POP accounts. In this section of the guide, you will be learning how to set up the Mail App and maximize it. So, let's get started!

How to Add Your Email Accounts to Mail app

You probably have many email accounts and you may wish to add these accounts to the Mail app on your device.

Note: If you have already connected Microsoft account to the user account on your device, then Windows should automatically add your Microsoft account to the Mail app. However, you will still need to follow the steps I am about to mention to add other email accounts to the Mail App.

The email accounts you can add to Mail app include Google Mail, Yahoo Mail, iCloud, Exchange, Outlook among others.

To add an email account:

- Click the **Start** button located at the lower left corner of the screen.

- On the Start menu, click on **Mail.**

- If you are starting the Mail app for the first time, click on **Get Started.**

- Click on **Add account** button to add a new account.

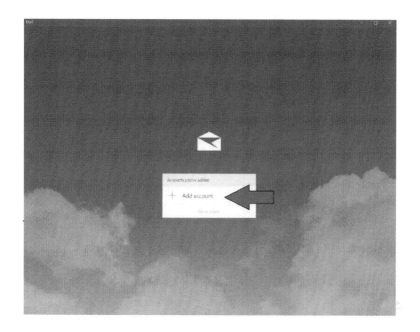

- Fill in the details by typing in your email address and password and then click on **Sign-in.** If you want to add a Gmail account, tap **Google.**

- That is all! Mail adds your email account to the Mail Account.

- After the whole setup, just click on **Go to Inbox.**

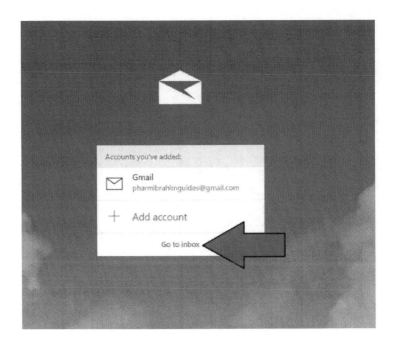

Please note that you may be prompted to select what you want to share with Windows during the Mail app setup process, I will implore you to carefully go through all the items on the list before clicking **Allow.**

Tip:

If you are not starting the Mail app for the first time and you wish to add another account, click **Settings** button and then click **Manage Accounts** (as shown below).

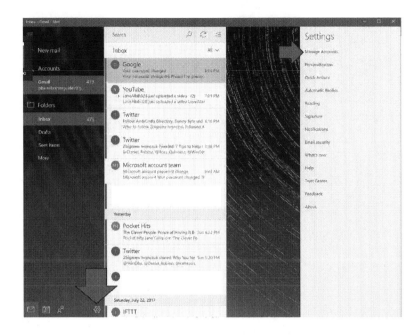

Click **Add account** and then choose an account from the list that appears.

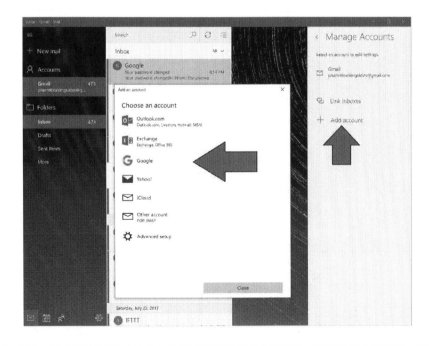

Special Note on Adding Exchange Account to Mail App

Following the instructions above might not be enough when you want to add your exchange account to Mail app, you may need an extra information. You may need to obtain from your Exchange administrator or provider the account server address, domain name, and username in addition to your email address and password.

How to Compose and Send an Email Message Using Mail App

You can easily send an email message to your friends or organization using the Mail App. In this section of the guide, we will be exploring how to compose an email message, how to save an email message as draft and how to send an email message. I will also take time to talk about how to format a text when composing an email message.

To send an email message:

- Tap on the plus **+ New mail** located at the top of the mail app.

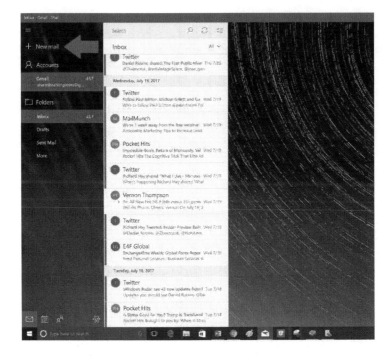

- Type in the email address of the recipient.

- To send a copy to another person, click on **Cc & Bcc** and type the person's email address in the **Cc/Bcc** field.

Tip: Cc means Carbon Copy. If you use Cc option to send message to many recipients, all the recipients will see the message and all other email addresses that have received the message. On the other hand, Bcc stand for Blind Carbon Copy. If you use Bcc option to send message to many recipients, all the recipients will see the message, but will not see other email addresses that have received the message.

- Type a subject for the message (The Subject section is immediately below the address section)

- Type in the body of the message.

- Tap **SEND** located at the top of the Mail app when you are done composing the message.

You can use the **Format** tab to perform the following actions:

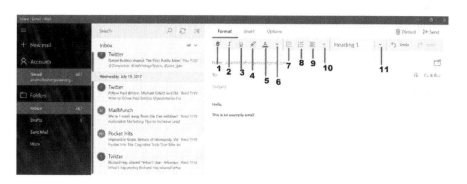

1. **Bold**: You can bold a part or your entire message using this feature. To bold a text, click the **B** icon.

2. **Italicize**: You can make your text appear italicized by clicking on the *I* icon.

3. **Underline**: Use the U icon to underline a text.

4. **Highlighter**: Use this button to highlight a text.

5. **Font Color**: Use this option to change the color of your text.

6. **Font formatting**: Use this option to add superscript/subscript to a text, strikethrough a text, change the font size or clear any formatting on a text.

7. **Bullets**: Use this button to add bullets to your texts.

8. **Numbering:** Use this button to add numbers to your texts.

9. **Alignment:** Use this button to align your texts.

10. **Paragraph**: Use this option to add special paragraphing features to your text just like you do with Microsoft Word. You can add Special Indent, Line Spacing, Space before Paragraph and Space after Paragraph using this option.

11. **Styles:** Use this tab to add headings, title, and quotes to your message.

Note: Before you can apply any of the formatting options above, you will need to select the text that you want to format. In addition, I will advise that you always use the formatting tab when composing an email; it makes your message easier to read.

- Use the **Insert** tab to perform the following:

1. **Files**: You can insert an attachment into your message by clicking on **Files**. This opens a dialog box. Locate and click on the file you want to attach and then click **Open** (located at the lower right corner of the dialog box).

2. **Table**: Use this option to insert a table into your message. To insert a table, position your cursor to where you want the table to appear, and then click on the **Table.** Use the following options to customize your table:

a) **Delete**: Use this option to delete a row, column, or the entire table.

b) **Insert:** Use this option to insert more columns or rows to your table.

c) **Style Options:** Use this option to add various styles to your table. *Please note that the style you choose may not be obvious if the table style option does not support it.*

d) **Table Styles:** Use this option to customize how the table will look like. This option determines whether your table will be a block of lines or something more elegant.

e) **Text:** Use this option to choose how the text in your table will look like. You can use this option to align the text the way you like. Please note that you will need to select a text before you can align it.

f) **Autofit:** Use this option to adjust contents or window.

g) **Cell Size:** Use this option to choose how the individual cell in the table will look like. Use

this option to adjust the width size of a row or column.

3. **Picture:** You can also insert an image or logo into your message. To insert an image, position the cursor where you want the picture to appear, and click **Pictures.** This opens a dialog box, locate and click the picture you want to insert and then click **Insert.** To adjust the picture size or crop the picture, click the picture and click on **Crop.** If you want to restore the image to the way it was, click the image and then click on **Reset Size.** In addition, you can also rotate a picture by clicking on **Rotate.**

4. **Link:** Use this option to add a link to your message.

Use the **Options** tab to check spellings in your message. You can also change the language selection for your message using this tab. In addition, use this tab to add level of importance to your message. You can choose between low importance and high importance.

1. **High Importance:** Use this button to give high importance to your message.

2. **Low Importance:** Use this button to give low importance to your message.

3. **Language:** Use this to select a language.

4. **Spelling:** Use this to check for spelling mistakes in your message.

5. **Proofing Options:** Use this to access more proofing options.

6. **Zoom:** Use to zoom your message.

7. **Find:** Use this to find for a word or phrase in your message.

Saving a Message as a Draft

If you don't wish to send your message right away, you can save it as a draft. Mail app saves your message automatically as a draft; all you need to do is to click elsewhere in the Mail Window. For example, you may click the **Inbox** while composing a message to prompt the Mail app to save your composition as a draft.

You can locate the draft message by clicking on **Drafts** usually located below **Inbox.** To delete a draft, open the draft message and click on **Discard** (located beside **Send**).

Understanding the Different Folders in Mail App

There are many folders under individual accounts in Mail App, these folders are highlighted below:

Inbox: Contain messages sent to your email address.

Draft: Contains those messages you have started composing but you have not finished up with.

Sent: This holds copies of the messages you have sent at one time or the other.

Outbox: This holds outgoing messages that are in the process of being sent.

Spam: This holds those messages that Mail has deemed to be unsolicited for. I will advise that you check your Spam email box before emptying it because your mail provider may mistakenly classify a message as spam.

Please note you may need to click on **More** button to access some of these folders.

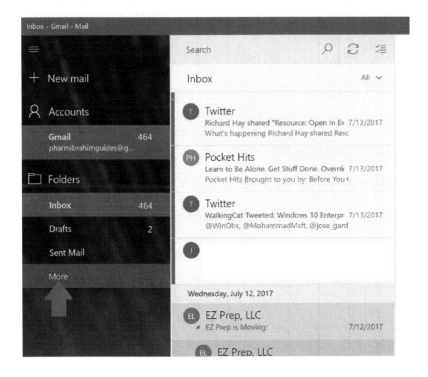

Mail App Keyboard Shortcuts

The following are some of the keyboard shortcuts that are available when using Mail app.

1. **Ctrl + B:** Bold

2. **Ctrl + U**: Underline

3. **Ctrl + I**: Italicize

4. **Ctrl + N**: New message

5. **Ctrl + Z**: Undo

6. **Ctrl + Y**: Redo

Managing a Received Email

One of the most important functions of any email app is the ability to receive incoming messages. By default, Mail app searches for new messages and alerts you when there is one.

New messages are either stored in Inbox or Spam folder and these are the two places to check if you are expecting an email.

To see if there is a new message, click on **Refresh** button located beside the Magnifying Lens icon at the upper part of the Mail app.

To read a message:

- Click on the subject of the message to open the message body in the preview pane.

- A bar appears beside messages that you have not yet read. See the picture below

- The attachment icon (paperclip icon) means that a message has an attachment.

- The Mail app allows you to perform the following options on a message in your inbox (see the red boxes in the screenshot below):

- **Reply:** Click this button to reply an email message. When you click this button, a new window appears. This window is similar to what appears when you click on **New mail** button but with a slight difference. This window already contains the recipient's name and the subject. In addition, the original message usually appears at the bottom of your reply for reference.

- **Reply All:** If the message in your inbox is addressed to several people, you can choose to reply all those people by clicking on **Reply All.** You can know whether an email is sent to many people by checking the email's **To** section.

- **Forward:** Use this option to send a copy of an email in your inbox to your friends or associates. When you click on the Forward button, a message windows with a subject line preceded by "FW:" appears. The original message's addresses (To and From), date, subject, attachment, and text are also included. In addition, you will have the option to fill in the email address of the person to whom you are sending the message. Use the **Cc & Bcc** (see page 161) to add other recipients (if any).

- **Delete:** Use this option to move the email to the trash bin.

- **Set Flag:** You can use this option to mark an email so that you may deal with it at a later time.

- **Three Dots (More) Icon:** Click on this icon to gain access to options like **Move** and **Print**.

The **Move** option allows you to change the location of an email from one place to another.

Hint: When you open the Mail app inbox to check a mail, the name of the sender is usually displayed on the top of the message pane. To see the email address for whoever sent the message, click the name. A pop-box will show up displaying the email address.

In addition, if you need more working space, you can open an email message in a new window. To do this, click on the icon shown below:

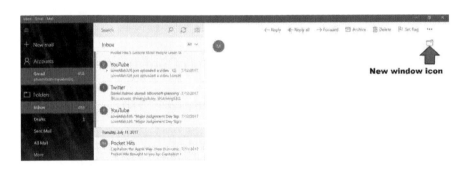

New window icon

How to Open and Save an Attachment in Mail App

The email with an attachment will have a paper clip icon displayed next to the address of the sender when you check your message inbox.

To open an attachment:

1. Click the message that has the attachment, as indicated by a paper clip.

2. When the message opens, click the attachment that you want to open.

3. The file then opens in the appropriate program. If your PC is not having an appropriate program to open the attachment, you may see a message like, "Windows can't open this type of file". In a situation like this, you will need to install the appropriate program for the type of file. You may ask the person that sent the message about which program to use to open the attachment.

To save an attachment:

1. Repeat the first two steps above. Then right click the attachment that you want to save and choose **Save.**

2. The **Save As** dialog box appears. Click the folder where you want to store the file. You can edit the name of attachment using the **File name** section.

3. Click **Save** when you are done.

How to Restore a Deleted Message

You may change your mind after deleting a message and may wish to restore it. To restore a deleted message:

1. Click **More.**

2. Click **Trash** or **Deleted Items**

3. Right click the message that you want to restore and select **Move.**

4. Click **Inbox.** You may also choose another folder if you like.

How to Create a Folder in Mail App

You may want to create a folder to get your email more organized. Creating a new folder helps you de-clutter your message inbox. By saving different emails to different folders, you make it easier to locate a message in the future.

To create a folder:

1. Click **More**.

2. Click the new folder icon (the plus icon).

3. Enter a name for the folder in the white box that appears and press enter.

To move a message to the newly created folder, right click the message and choose **Move,** then select the name of the folder from the list.

To rename your folder, right click the folder you want to rename and then select **Rename**. Enter a new name and press enter when you are done.

How to Change the Background of Mail App

You may want to select a different background image for the Mail app. To do this, open the Mail app, click on the **Settings** icon (located at the left lower part of the app), and click **Personalization.** Under **Background Picture,** pick an image. In addition, you can click on **Browse...** and choose an image from your library. Then click on **Open.**

Managing the Settings Options

Some of the options under Mail Settings have already been discussed. But let me briefly explain some of the options that have not been discussed.

Note: To access the Mail app settings, click on the settings icon located at the lower left corner of the app.

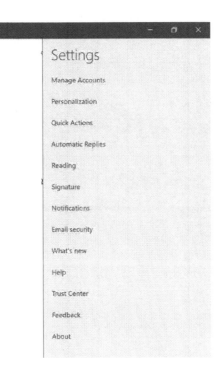

Quick Actions: The options under this tab include:

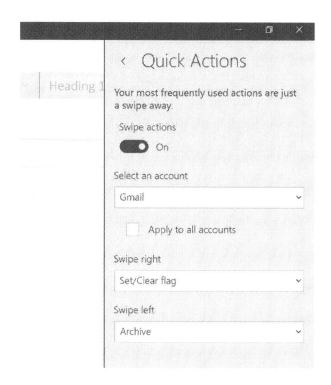

- **Swipe actions**: If you do not want to use a gesture on your Surface, select **Off** under this option.

- **Select an account**: If you have multiple accounts, you can select the account to apply the settings to. In addition, you may select **Apply to all accounts** if you want to apply the settings to all the accounts.

- **Swipe right:** Use this option to select what windows will do when you swipe right on a message.

- **Swipe left:** Use this option to select what windows will do when you swipe left on a message.

Automatic replies: If your email provider supports it, you can use this method to reply an email automatically.

Reading: You can use the reading option to **Auto-open next item, Mark item as read,** use **Caret Browsing** and many more.

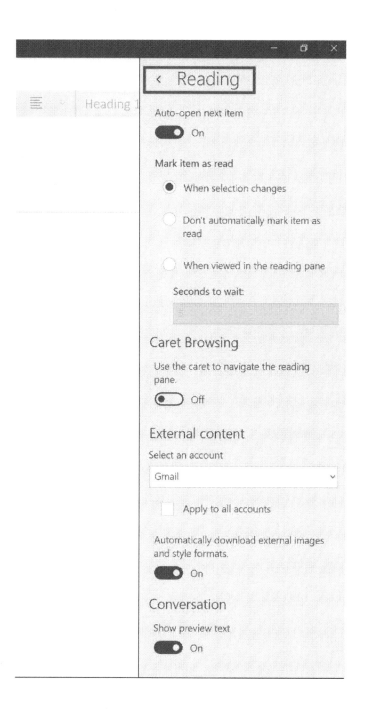

Signature: Use this option to tell Mail app what signature to include in a message. You can also edit signature message using this option. If you don't want to see any signature, select **Off** under this option.

Note: An email signature is a text that appears by default after the body of your message. You may set your email signature to be your name or your brand.

Other settings options are:

Notifications: You can use this tab to manage the notification settings.

Email Security: Through this, you can access security options. Please note that your account provider may not support this option.

What's new: Use this option to learn more about new things you can do with Mail App.

Help: Click this to get Microsoft help.

Trust Center: Microsoft uses this option to give you locally relevant content.

Feedback: Click this option if you like to give a feedback.

About: Click this option to know more about the Mail app.

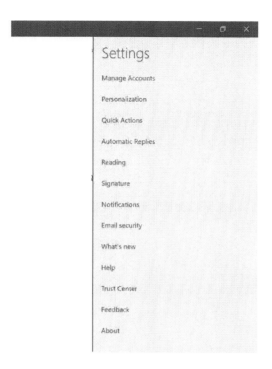

How to Remove the Default Email Signature in Mail App

To remove an email signature in Mail app, please refer to page 181 and 182.

Conclusion

Mail App is a cool app and I will really love that you get the best out of it. Using this guide will not only get you started, but it will also get you going with this app.

Personal Information

Contacts

This app allows you to create and manage a list of your personal or business contacts. You can save names, mobile phone numbers, home phone numbers, email address, and more.

To create a contact:

1. Select the search box in the taskbar, enter **People**, and in the search results, tap **People**.

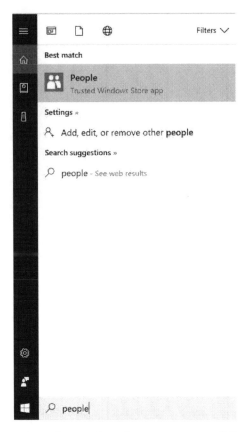

2. Click on + icon located at the upper part of the screen.

3. Choose a place to save the contact.

Choose account

Choose an account and we'll save your
new contacts there from now on. You'll
always have the option to use a different
account whenever you add a contact.

Microsoft account

Gmail

Close

4. Fill in the details and save the contact by clicking on **Save**.

5. To add more information such as website address, click on
Other and then select an option from the list that appears.

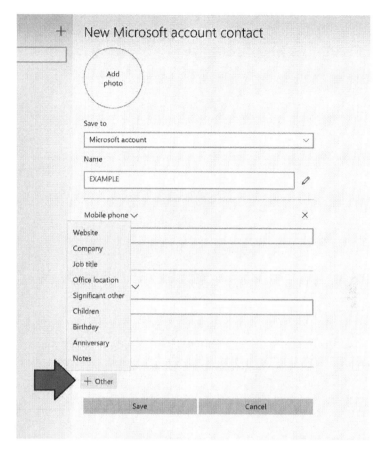

Hint: To search for a contact, open the **People** app and click search bar, and start typing a name. The list filters as you type. In addition, if you have your contacts backup on Google, your Surface should automatically add them to People's app after you signed into Gmail account using the Mail app that came with your Surface device.

To manage a contact:

1. Select the search box in the Taskbar, enter **People**, and in the search results, tap **People**.

2. Click on a contact from the list.

3. Use the onscreen icons to perform different tasks of your choice.

 a. To delete a contact, click the menu icon (...) located at the upper right corner of the screen and click **Delete.**

 b. To edit a contact, click and enter the desired details.

 c. To pin a contact, click the pin icon located beside the edit icon. Alternatively, to pin a contact to the Start, right-click a contact, and select **Pin to Start**.

 d. To share a contact, click the menu icon (...) located at the upper right corner of the screen and click **Share contact.**

 e. To access settings, click the setting icon located at the lower left corner of the screen.

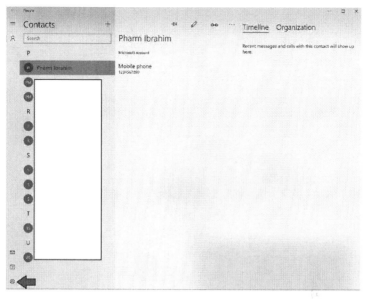

f. To link a contact, click ⊖⊙ and click **Choose a contact to link** and then click the contact to be linked. Linking two contacts is important if you have separate entries for the same contact from different social networking services or email accounts. To unlink a contact, select the contact you want to unlink, and click ⊖⊙ . Then select the contact you want to unlink from, and click **Unlink**.

Sorting contact list

You can sort contacts on your device by first name or last name.

1. Select the search box in the Taskbar, enter **People**, and in the search results, tap **People**.

2. Click the setting icon 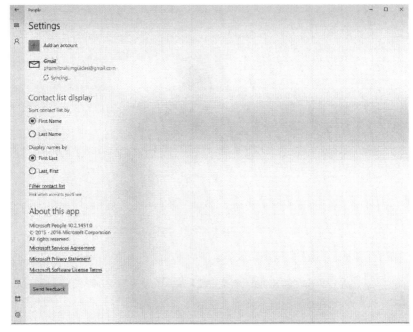 located at the lower left corner of the screen.

3. Select **First Name** or **Last Name**.

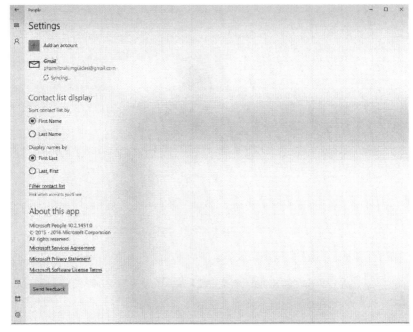

Tip: You can add an email account to **People** app so that you can sync the contacts (if any) on that email account with the app. To do this, while on the **People** app, click the setting icon located at the lower left. Then click **Add an account.**

Accessibility Features – The Special features for easy usage

Accessibility services are special features for those with physical challenges. It also provides you the opportunity to control your Surface in a special way.

To access the accessibility options:

- Swipe in from the right edge of the screen, click **All settings**.
- Click **Ease of Access** and then click your desired settings. Then click on any of the following:

1. Narrator/Screen Reader

This option allows you to hear what is happening on the screen as you touch/interact with the screen.

To turn on the screen reader, click **Narrator** and then click the switch next to **Narrator**. When in the Narrator screen, you can use the onscreen options to customize the Narrator's feature. However, please note that the default settings might just be what you need.

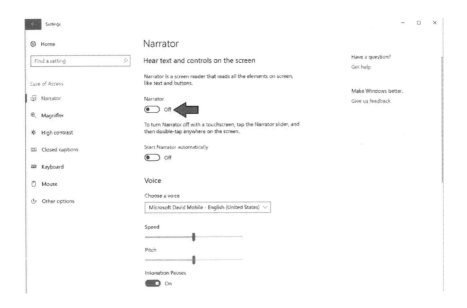

Using the screen reader/narrator

- **To explore/select menus/items/icons on the screen:** Click on an item to select it. The screen reader read what you have selected to you. Then double click to open the item you have selected.

To turn off the screen reader/narrator:

1. Swipe in from the right edge of the screen, click **All settings**.
2. Click **Ease of Access** and then click **Narrator.**
3. Then click the switch next to **Narrator** to switch it off.

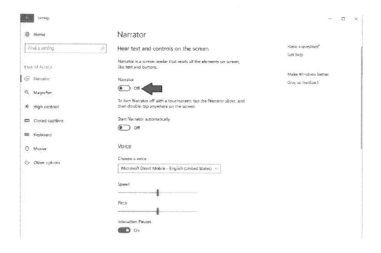

2. Screen Magnifier

This option allows you to use certain gestures to magnify your screen so that you may better see what is on the screen.

To turn on screen magnifier, click **Magnifier** and then click the switch next to **Magnifier**.

When the Screen magnifier is on, you can perform any of these actions:

i. To scroll down or scroll up while viewing an item: Use the trackpad on the keyboard. You may also use the arrow keys on the keyboard to scroll up or down. Please note that the keyboard is sold separately if you are using Surface Pro.

ii. To disable screen magnifier: Look for the lens icon
and click on it. Then select the close (**X**) icon to close the screen
reader.

3. High Contrast

This option allows you to choose how things appear on the
screen of your Surface. You can choose from available
contrasts. I will advise that you try various contrast settings
available in order to choose the one you like best. When you
are done choosing a theme (see the red arrow below), click on
Apply.

4. **Closed caption**

Closed captioning is a feature that allows hearing impaired individuals have a visual display (usually in form of text) of audio portion of a program. It can be likened to subtitling. If you make a mistake when customizing closed caption settings, you can always restore it back to default by clicking on **Restore to defaults**.

Tip: If you do not know much about Closed captioning, the default settings might just be enough.

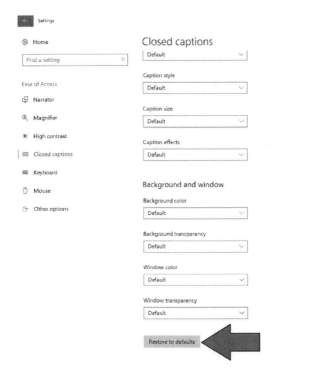

5. **Keyboard**

This option allows you to manage the keyboard settings for easy access. For example, you can use the settings under keyboard, to tell your device to make sound when **Cap Lock**, **Num Lock** or **Scroll Lock** is pressed.

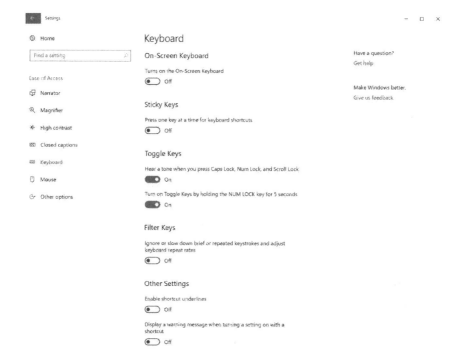

Settings

⚙ Home

Find a setting

Ease of Access

🗐 Narrator

🔍 Magnifier

☀ High contrast

🔠 Closed captions

⌨ Keyboard

🖱 Mouse

🗗 Other options

Keyboard

On-Screen Keyboard

Turns on the On-Screen Keyboard

◉━ Off

Sticky Keys

Press one key at a time for keyboard shortcuts

◉━ Off

Toggle Keys

Hear a tone when you press Caps Lock, Num Lock, and Scroll Lock

━◉ On

Turn on Toggle Keys by holding the NUM LOCK key for 5 seconds

━◉ On

Filter Keys

Ignore or slow down brief or repeated keystrokes and adjust keyboard repeat rates

◉━ Off

Other Settings

Enable shortcut underlines

◉━ Off

Display a warning message when turning a setting on with a shortcut

◉━ Off

Have a question?
Get help

Make Windows better.
Give us feedback

6. Mouse

This option allows you to manage the mouse settings for easy access. For example, you can use the settings under **Mouse** to customize both mouse pointer size and color.

7. Other Options

Other Options allow you to manage settings like Windows background, cursor thickness, touch feedback, among others. I will advise that you try various settings under this tab in order to get used to them.

Settings

⊟ ☐ ✕

⊚ Home

| Find a setting | 🔎 |

Ease of Access

🖵 Narrator

🔍 Magnifier

☀ High contrast

🔳 Closed captions

🖩 Keyboard

🖰 Mouse

🕃 Other options

Other options

Visual options

Play animations in Windows

On

Show Windows background

On

Show notifications for

| 5 seconds ∨ |

Cursor thickness

| I | ●━━━━━━━━━━━━━━━━━━━━━━

Visual notifications for sound

| None ∨ |

Touch feedback

Show visual feedback when I touch the screen

On

Use darker, larger visual feedback (ideal for presentations)

Off

Audio options

Mono audio

Off

Have a question?
Get help

Make Windows better.
Give us feedback

201

TOOLS

Cortana

Getting started with Cortana

Cortana is a trained virtual assistant that has been built to answer questions, and let you interact with your device in a special way.

To get started with Cortana:

- Click in the search box. If prompted to agree to terms and conditions, read the terms and conditions and then tap I agree.

- Type in a search term or say a search phrase.

Note: Although you may have to agree to the Cortana's privacy statement during the set up process, you can always choose how Cortana access your information. For example, you can adjust some settings under Notebook to limit the amount of information Cortana sends to Microsoft. Please see **Permission** on page 227 to find out more.

Speaking to Cortana

One of the ways you will interact with Cortana is by speaking to it. The other way will be to just type command into the search bar and hit **Enter**. There are few things to know when talking to Cortana so as to get the best experience.

To get Cortana into action, you will need to get its attention. To do that, perform any of the actions below:

1. Click on the microphone icon on the Start menu.

2. Alternatively, press **Windows logo key** + C. This will open the Cortana Listening box. You can then ask any question you want. Please note that you may need

to enable this feature before you can put it to use. To enable this;

- Click the search box on the Start menu.

- Click the Settings icon (see the red arrow below).

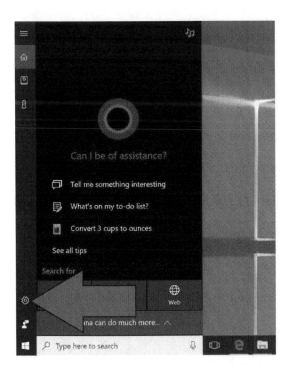

- Scroll down, next to **Keyboard shortcut,** select **On.**

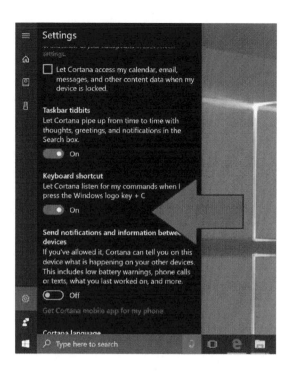

3. Alternatively, you can get Cortana's attention by saying **Hey Cortana!** However, you will need to enable this feature before you can put it to use. To enable **Hey Cortana** function:

 - Click the search box on the Start menu.

 - Click the Settings icon (see the red arrow below).

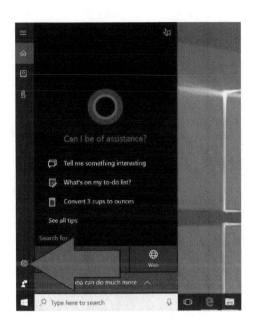

- Next to **Hey Cortana,** select **On**

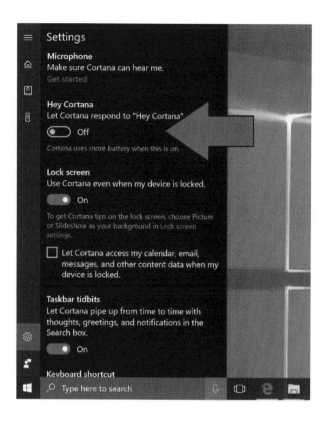

When Cortana is activated, it will respond by
saying **Listening** in the search box. Cortana will then give you
an answer on the search box immediately or open your web
browser. By default, Cortana will search the web using Bing
but you can always change this to Google. Please go to page
237 to know more.

In addition, occasionally, you may notice that the question
you asked Cortana is different from what it types into the
search box (what Cortana types into the search box is what it
thinks you have said).

What about Typing?

The interesting thing is that Cortana can also listen when you command it using your keyboard. You can type in command and get a similar result just as you will get by speaking to it. This is a great feature especially if you can't speak to Cortana for one reason or the other e.g. if you are in a noisy place or your microphone is not working properly.

For example, you can get a result of what Cortana can do for you by typing **What can I say** into the search box (located on the start menu) and then hit **Enter**. This is similar to the result you will get when you say **What can I say** to Cortana.

Getting What You Want from Cortana

There are many things you can ask Cortana to do for you, and before you finish reading this guide you will learn how to effectively interact with it.

I will like to mention that interacting with Cortana is not an examination (so there is nothing like cheating) and you can always get a list of what it can do for you by typing or speaking **What can I say** or **What can you do** and then clicking a category from the list that appears.

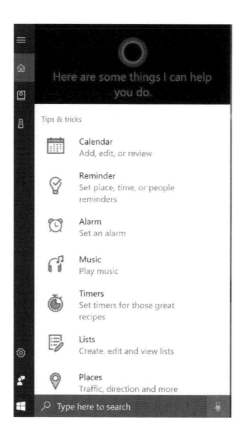

If you are speaking to it, please don't forget that you will first need to press the microphone button as described in the section above. Alternatively, if you have enabled the feature, you may also say **Hey Cortana** to get its attention. Asking **what can I say** is a good way to help yourself anytime you get stuck on how to use this virtual assistant.

Using Cortana to open Apps or Programs

One of those things you will want to use Cortana to do is accessing your apps. You can quickly open an app by saying **Open** and then mention the name of the app. For example, to open Settings, say or type **Open settings.** To open calculator, say **Open calculator**.

You may also say **Launch settings** instead of **Open settings.**

In addition, you may give a more specific command like **Open notification settings** to go to notification settings. Say **Launch Wi-Fi Settings** to open the Wi-Fi settings. To turn off airplane mode, say **Turn off airplane mode** and so on.

Using Cortana with Calendar

One of the fantastic features that Cortana can do for you is making an appointment. This personal assistant is fully integrated with your device's Calendar making it easy for it to make appointments for you.

With just few commands you can get Cortana to put an event or appointment into your calendar. **To do this:**

1. Press **Windows logo Key** + **C** or click the microphone icon on the search bar to get Cortana's attention. It will respond by typing **listening** in the search box.

2. Then say whatever you want to include in the Calendar. For example, you can say any of the following:

 - Appointment with Clinton for Monday at 1 p.m.

 - Be in a conference with John at 10 a.m. on Sunday.

 - Remind me to fix my car at 9 p.m. tonight. Please note that you can also say all the examples given above in other ways, the most important thing is to get Cortana to understand what you are saying.

 - When it has got the information, the Calendar will appear on the Start menu. You can then click on **Add** or say **Yes** if you are satisfied with the response. If not, say **No** or **Cancel.**

You can also make changes to your calendar using Cortana. **To do this**:

1. Repeat the first step above.

2. Then say what you want it to change. For example, you may say any of the following:

 - Change the meeting schedule for 1 p.m. to 4 p.m.

 - Move my appointment from 5 p.m. to 7 p.m.

As at the time of writing this guide, it appears that you may not be able to change your reminders using Cortana, you may need to enter the changes yourself. However, please note that you can use Cortana to set reminders.

In addition, you can check how your calendar looks like. To do this, click the microphone button and say, **"What is on my calendar today?"** Or say, **"any appointment today**?" Or just any variant. Note that you can also ask Cortana about your calendar for a day in the future. To do this, say **"Any appointment tomorrow"** or say, **"Any appointment on November 1st."**

Note: In case, Cortana sets a wrong appointment, you can edit it using your keyboard instead of trying to speak another word to it. Editing any misinformation with keyboard appears smarter and faster.

In addition, instead of speaking, you may type any of the commands mentioned above into the search box to get a similar result.

Using Cortana to set Reminders

There are probably many things going through your mind and it will be quite interesting if you can get a personal assistant to assist in remembering some of your duties. Fortunately, Cortana can help you in this regard.

To set a reminder using Cortana:

1. Press **Windows logo Key + C** or click the microphone icon on the search bar to get Cortana's attention. It will respond by typing **listening** in the search box.

2. Then say whatever you want to set a reminder for. For example, you can say the following:

 - Remind me to fix the car by 3 p.m.

- Remind me to drop the cake at the restaurant.

- Remind me to pick my daughter at 4 p.m.

- Remind me to call Clinton at 1 p.m., and so on.

3. When it has grabbed the information, the reminder will appear. You can then click on **Add** or say **Yes** if you are satisfied with the response. If not, say **No** or **Cancel.**

Please note that it is probably not compulsory that you put **remind** in every statement as I did above, but I will advise that you to do so whenever you can. This is because it will help Cortana to easily get what you are saying and avoid any confusion.

Note: In case, Cortana sets a wrong reminder, you can edit it using your keyboard instead of trying to speak another word to it. Editing any misinformation with keyboard appears smarter and faster.

Using Cortana with Alarm

You can also set an alarm using this personal assistant. **To do this**:

1. Repeat the first step mentioned above.

2. Say the time for alarm. For example, you can say: "**set an alarm for 1 p.m. every Wednesday**" or "**alarm for 1 p.m. every Wednesday**".

3. When it has grabbed the information, the alarm will appear and it will tell you that it has set the alarm.

Downside: As at the time of writing this guide, it appears that you may not be able to set an alarm for a particular date, you can try setting a reminder in such a case.

Using Cortana with Clock

You can ask Cortana what your local time is. In addition, it can also tell you the time in a specific place.

1. Press **Windows logo Key + C** or click the microphone icon on the search bar to get Cortana's attention. It will respond by typing **listening** in the search box.

2. Then say, **"What is the time"** or say, **"what is the time in New York"**

Using Cortana to Get Flight Information

You can also use this virtual assistant to get information about a flight. This is a smarter way to know when an airplane will take off.

For example, you can say **Flight status of Delta 400** to get the flight information about this particular flight.

Using Cortana with Weather App

To know about the weather condition of a place, just say **"What's the weather going to be today"**. You may also know about the weather condition of a place by asking **"What is the weather of New York today."**

Using Cortana with Mail App

You can instruct Cortana to compose an email for you. To do this:

1. Press **Windows logo Key** + **C** or click the microphone

 icon on the search bar to get Cortana's attention. It

 will respond by typing **listening** in the search box.

2. Then say the subject and the person you want to email. For example, you can say:

 - Email Clinton about the meeting.

 - Email Clinton and Steve about the budget.

 - Send an urgent email to Steve about our plan.

The interesting thing is that you can type some of the commands given above into the search box and get the same results.

Please note that you will usually have to include one or more information before you send the email. For example, you may need to type the body of the email yourself. You can click **Continue in your email app** link to finish the email process.

Using Cortana with Map App

You can also use the Cortana to search the map. This virtual assistant is fully integrated with the Map app on your device. **To get how the map of a place looks like**:

1. Repeat the first step above.

2. Then say the map of an area you want to get. For example, you may say:

 - Map of Seattle.

 - Show me the map of Seattle.

What about Math?

Cortana can also help you with some mathematical calculations and conversion. For example, you can tell Cortana **"What is the square root of four"**. You may also say **"convert foot to centimeter"** or **"What is the exchange rate between dollars and pounds"** and so on. As I have said, the most important thing is to make sure Cortana get the message you are trying to get across.

Using Cortana to get definitions

You can quickly check for the meaning of a word by asking Cortana. For example, you may say **"What is the meaning of flabbergasted"** or just say **"Meaning of flabbergasted"**

Note: Sometime, Cortana will display the answer of what you are asking for in your Web browser and not on the search pane.

Using Cortana with Microsoft Edge

You can also use this personal assistant when using your Microsoft Edge browser.

While using your Edge browser, you can use Cortana in the following ways:

- **Address bar search**: When you type in some specific phrases into the address bar on Edge browser, you can put Cortana to work. For example, to check the weather of New York, type in **Weather 10024.** This will give you the New York weather information even before you hit **Enter** key.

- **More info about a phrase**: If you are reading an article, and you encounter a word or phrase that is difficult, you can quickly ask Cortana. Just select the text and right click on it. Then choose **Ask Cortana.** See the red arrow below.

Funny sides of Cortana

One of the main features that is cool about Cortana is its ability to give a reply in a funny manner. This all depends on what you ask. Some of the questions you can ask to get funny replies are given below:

- Question: Do you sleep?

- Cortana: I never sleep, sleep is for ambulatory carbon-based being.

- Question: Do you eat?

- Cortana: I can only consume things that come in bytes.

- Question: Do you like your job?

- Cortana: I am tailor-made for this job.

- Question: Do you have a brain?

- Cortana: Thinking, thinking... I don't think so.

- Question: Do you cook?

- Cortana: Even if I could, you would be smart not to eat it. I'm better at looking up recipes.

The list of questions you can ask Cortana to get lovely replies goes on like that. As I have said, it all depends on the type of question you ask this virtual machine sitting on your device.

Cortana's Card and the Notebook

The notebook is like a special note pad where Cortana stores information about you.

On the other hand, the Cortana card is what appears when you click the search box (before saying or typing anything). This usually includes news headlines, weather, restaurant recommendations and so on. An example of Cortana card is shown below:

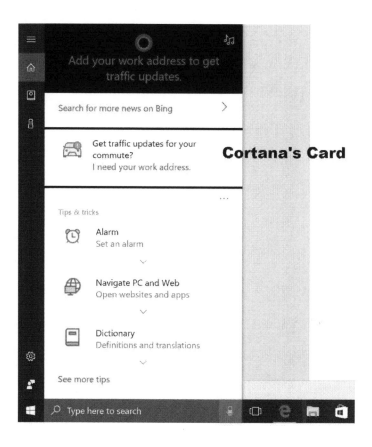

Cortana's Card

Hint: When viewing the Cortana's card in Cortana's pane, click on the three dots icon (…) located beside the individual cards to quickly manage the settings. See the screenshot below.

Interestingly, you can tell Cortana how you want the cards to be displayed to you. You can customize which kind of cards appear in its panel. To do this, please follow the steps below:

1. Click the search box and click the Notebook icon .

2. Then click on any of the cards that you want to customize. These cards include:

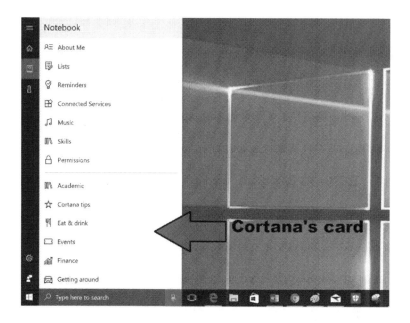

- **Academic:** Use this option to tell Cortana to give you an academic information.

- **Cortana Tip**: Use this option to tell Cortana whether you want it to display tips to you when you get stuck when speaking to it.

- **Eat & Drink**: You can use this option to tell this virtual assistant what type of information to give you on food and drink.

- **Events**: Use this option to tell Cortana what you will like to know about local events.

- **Finance**: Use this option to tell Cortana which stock to track.

- **Getting around**: Use this option to manage your traffic.

Please note that there are still more options under Cortana's card, and I will advise that you go through all of them individually to familiarize yourself with them. Most of the options under Cortana's card are self-explanatory and I believe you will get used to them easily.

*More importantly, if for one reason or the other, you don't want Cortana to get much information about you, then make sure you only turn **On** the features you are pleased with under the Cortana's card. Don't just turn **On** all the features if you don't need them.*

Others features in Cortana's Notebook

Other than Cortana's card, we have few more features under Cortana's notebook and they include (but not limited to):

- **About Me**: Use this option to change the name Cortana calls you. You also have the option to enter your favorites under the favorite tab. The favorite tab allows you to enter information relating to places you visit often. Use the + icon to add favorites. When you are done with the settings under this tab, click the Notebook icon to go back to the Notebook settings.

- **List**: This option allows you to manage your to-do list, grocery list and shopping list.

- **Reminders**: This option allows you to manage your reminders.

- **Connected Services**: Use this option to connect service like **Office 365** to Cortana so that Cortana can serve you better.

- **Skills**: You can use the skill tab to give Cortana more functions.

- **Permission**: Use this tab to manage what information Cortana can access.

Cortana's Settings

The settings tab allows you to manage Cortana's functions. To access Cortana's settings, click settings icon.

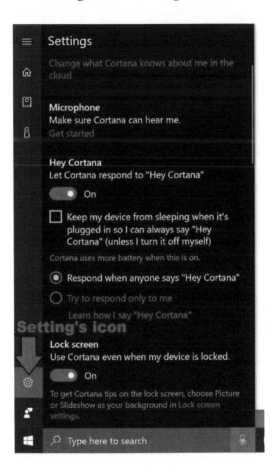

The settings include:

Microphone: Use this tab to troubleshoot microphone so that Cortana can hear you.

Cortana's Off/On Switch: Use this option to completely turn off Cortana. If this switch is moved to the **Off** position, you will not be able to use any of the Cortana's features.

Hey Cortana: Use this option to control whether Cortana will respond to **Hey Cortana.** When this feature is **On**, you will be able to get this virtual assistant attention by saying **Hey Cortana.** This feature appears cool but may also consume your device battery. It is better off if you want to save your battery power.

Lock Screen: When enabled, this option allows you to use the Cortana while your device is locked.

Taskbar tidbits: Use this option to control what appears on the search bar on the taskbar. When this option is enabled, Cortana can give you thoughts, greetings and notifications.

Keyboard shortcut: When this option is enabled, you will be able to get Cortana's attention by pressing **Windows logo key + C**.

Send notifications and information between devices: When this option is enabled, you can get information from your other devices running Cortana.

Cortana Language: Use this option to change Cortana's language.

My device history: When enabled, your search result is enhanced.

My search history: When enabled, your search result is enhanced.

SafeSearch Settings: Click on this option to manage Bing search settings.

Other Privacy settings: Use this to get access to extra privacy options

*Note: If for one reason or the other, you don't want Cortana to get much information about you, then make sure you only turn **On** the features/settings you are pleased with.*

Learn more about Cortana & Search: Click on this option to get access to **Cortana, Search, and privacy: FAQ** webpage.

How to Completely Clear Cortana's Cloud History (Stored Information)

To erase whatever Cortana has stored in the cloud, click the search bar on the taskbar and then click on the settings icon

. Click on **Change what Cortana knows about me in the cloud** (located at the top of the screen). Scroll down and tap **Clear.**

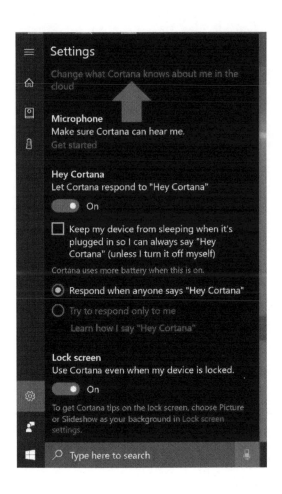

Tip: To clear Cortana's search history, click the search bar on

the Taskbar and then click on the settings icon 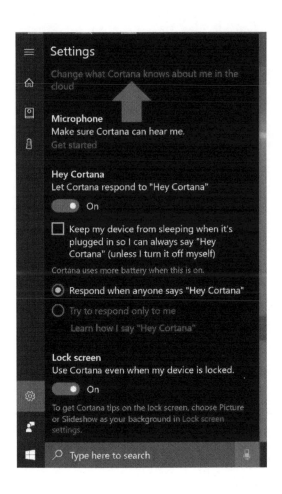. Then

scroll down and click on **Clear my device history**.

Forcing Cortana to Use Other Browsers

By default, Cortana is customized to use Edge browser to search for information online, but there is a way to change these settings. To do this:

1. Download and install the app called **KB EdgeDeflector_install.exe** by following **this link** https://github.com/da2x/EdgeDeflector/releases/tag/v1.0.1.0

2. Tap the search box on the Taskbar and enter a search phrase, for example, you may type **how about Samsung s8** and press **Enter.**

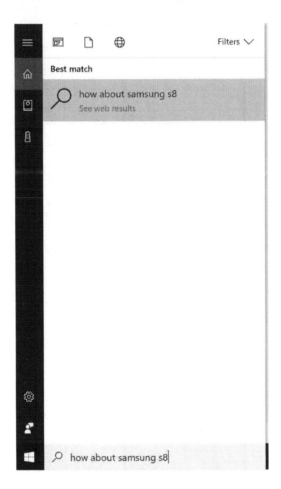

3. Select **EdgeDeflector** from the dialogue box that appears and tap **OK.**

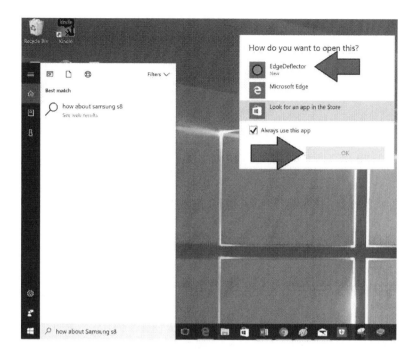

4. Type "**Default app settings**" into the search bar on the Start menu and press **Enter.**

5. Scroll down until you find **Web browser**, click on this and select Firefox or just any other browser from the list.

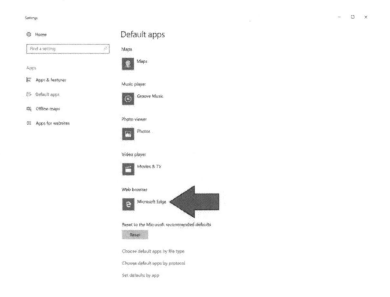

You are now fine, Cortana will now begin to use the web browser you have chosen instead of Edge browser.

Note: If the dialogue box mentioned in step **3** does not appear, make sure your default browser is still Edge Browser. You can only change the default browser after you have successfully performed the instruction on step 3 above. To know if your default browser is still Edge browser, go to **Settings > Apps & features > Default apps > Microsoft Edge.**

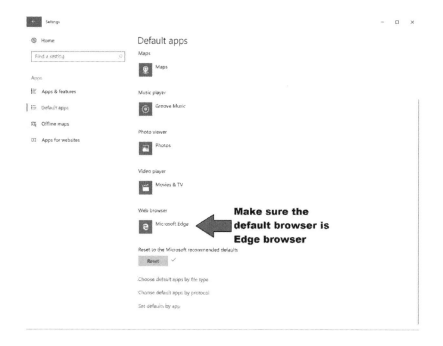

Changing the Cortana and Bing partnership

By default, Cortana uses Bing to search for information online, but you can force it to use Google.

To do this:

Make your default browser is Mozilla Firefox by following the steps mentioned in the preceding section. Thereafter, install **Bing-Google** (https://addons.mozilla.org/En-us/firefox/addon/bing-google-1/) extension.

That is all, all your searches will now be redirected to Google.

Please do note that the search results shown in the Taskbar pane will still be carried out by Bing. Only the searches carried out by web browser will be carried out by Google.

Other things you may like to know about Cortana

One cool feature that not many people know about is the fact that you can completely hide the Cortana icon/panel. You may also reduce the Cortana search bar to just a small icon. **To do this**:

1. Right click on the Cortana's search box and then click on **Cortana.**

2. Then choose any of the following:

 - **Hidden:** Choose this option to completely hide this virtual assistant.

 - **Show Cortana icon:** Choose this option to reduce Cortana to a small icon on the Taskbar.

 - **Show Search box:** Choose this option to display the Cortana search box. This is the default.

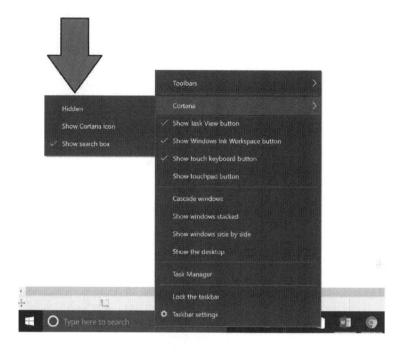

Troubleshooting Cortana

Although much efforts have been put into making this virtual assistant, I am quite sure that Cortana will misbehave at one time or the other. When this happens, there are few things to do.

- **Ensure that you are connected to a strong network**: If you have a bad or no internet connection, Cortana may not work properly. Therefore, the first thing to check

when Cortana starts to misbehave is the internet connection.

- **Use the keyboard**: You may need to use the keyboard to pass your message to Cortana if you find out that it is not getting your speech. Many of what you say (If not all) can also be typed into the Cortana's search bar.

- **Try to Restart Your Surface**: If you find out that what I have mentioned above does not work, you may try restarting your Surface because it may be that it is your Surface that is confused and not Cortana.

Conclusion

Cortana is like a learning machine and it is being improved upon. If you are having difficulty passing your message across to it, you may try typing some of your commands into the search box. I strongly believe you will know how to use it more as time goes on. Don't forget that Rome was not built in a day.

The Calendar App

Creating schedules and more with the Calendar

Your Surface provides you with a **Calendar** app to help you organize your schedules and tasks more conveniently and effectively. You can create schedules and add events.

Number	Function
1.	Click this icon to move from one calendar month/week to another.
2.	Click this icon to move from one calendar month/week to another.
3.	Click this to go to today's date.
4.	Click this icon to access the **Day view**.

5.	Click this icon to access the **Week view.**
6.	Click this icon to see the **Month view.**
7.	Click this icon to access the **Year view.**
8.	Click this to access extra features like print and sync.
9.	Click any day to create an event corresponding to that day
10.	Click the **settings icon** to manage your accounts, personalize your Calendar app, manage your Calendar and Weather settings, view help information, and give feedback on your experience.
11.	Click this icon to access your contacts.
12.	Click this icon to go back to Calendar view.
13.	Click this icon to go to the Mail app.
14.	Click this icon to add calendars from other parts of the world. **Tip**: *If you like to know the holidays in a country, then add the country to your calendar using this icon.*
15.	Click the checkbox to select or deselect an account/option. When you deselect an account, the calendar

	events/appointments/reminders from that account may not be shown.
16.	Select this checkbox if you want Calendar app to show your reminders.
17.	Click this icon to add a new event.
18.	Click this icon to expand or collapse the day/week/month view.

> **To create an event**

1. Select the search box in the Taskbar, enter **Calendar**, and in the search results, select **Calendar**.

2. Click on the '**+**' icon at the upper side of the screen and enter the event name, date and time and other details.

3. To add number of times to repeat the event and set a reminder, click the **Repeat** icon located at the upper side of the screen.

4. To create a private appointment/event, click ⌂ located at the upper side of the screen.

5. When you are done, click save icon located at the upper side of the screen.

Tip: To send a meeting invitation or notify people about an event, when creating an event, click the box next to **People** (located at the upper right part of the screen). Type the name or the email address of those people you want to message. Please note that you may only be able to send meeting invitations to contact(s) who have an email address defined in the contact details on your **People** app.

Note: When there is an upcoming event in the calendar, you should receive a reminder.

> ➤ **To view an event/schedule**

1. Select the search box in the Taskbar, enter **Calendar**, and in the search results, click **Calendar**.
2. Click on the day of the event, and then click on an event to view.

> ➤ **To change calendar view**

1. Select the search box in the Taskbar, enter **Calendar**, and in the search results, tap **Calendar**.
2. Choose the right view using the onscreen icons. See the picture on page 241.

➢ **To edit or delete an event**

1. Select the search box in the Taskbar, enter **Calendar**, and in the search results, tap **Calendar**.

2. Click on the day of the event, and then click on the event's name.

3. When you are done, click save icon⌘ .

4. To delete an appointment/event, click 🗑 .

➢ **Add an account to calendar app**

You can put your calendars from different accounts in Calendar app. **To get this done**;

1. Select the search box in the Taskbar, enter **Calendar**, and in the search results, tap **Calendar**.

2. Click the settings icon ⚙ located at the lower side of the screen.

3. Click **Manage Accounts.**

4. Click **+Add account**.

5. Choose an account, and follow the onscreen instructions.

➢ **View or Hide Calendars**

If you have multiple calendars (calendars from Yahoo mail, Facebook etc.) synced to your Surface, you can select which ones to display by following the steps below:

1. Select the search box in the Taskbar, enter **Calendar**, and in the search results, tap **Calendar**.

2. Click the menu icon ☰ (if necessary), and then click the checkbox next to the calendar you want to display.

Please note that when a calendar is hidden, the calendar events/appointments/reminders are not shown. This means that you may need to unhide the calendar to view all events/appointments associated with it.

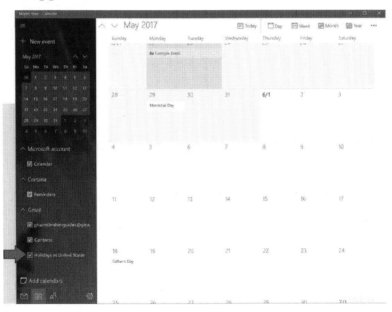

File Explorer App

File Explorer is an app that allows you to easily access files that are available on your Surface.

To access **File Explorer**, select the search box in the Taskbar, and begin to type **File Explorer**, and in the search results, choose **File Explorer**.

The **File Explorer** app contains **four main** tabs:

1. **File** tab: This tab allows you to open a new window of a selected file, access help information among others.

2. **Home** tab: This tab allows you to copy a file, delete a file, rename a file, check the file history (if turned on), move a file, among others. Please note that depending

on the file you have selected, some options may not be available under Home tab.

3. **Share** tab: This tab allows you to share, zip, email, print or fax a selected file. Please note that depending on the item you have selected, this tab may not be available.

4. **View** tab: This tab allows you to view a selected file as a list, large icons etc. You can also enable the preview pane using the View tab.

5. **Manage** tab: This tab allows you to rotate a selected file, set a file as background, and show a file in slide show. Please note that depending on the item you have selected; this tab may not be available. In addition, if you are in a slide show and you wish to exit it, just press the **Esc** button on the keyboard. Alternatively, right click and select **Exit**.

Note: You may need to first select a file, before you can access some features under File Explorer tab.

In addition, if you notice that any option is grayed out when you select an item, then that means that the option is not available for the selected item.

Tip: To quickly open another File explorer window while working on one, press **Ctrl + N.**

Connectivity

Homegroup

Homegroup allows you to share files and items between two or more Surfaces/PCs.

Creating a Homegroup Using a Wireless Router

It is quite easy to create a Homegroup on your Surface. To create a Homegroup, please follow the steps below:

- Connect your Surface to a wireless network (please make sure that it is a private network and not a public Wi-Fi). To search for an available network, click on the wireless icon ![wireless icon] on the Taskbar of your device.
- Select the search box in the Taskbar, enter **HomeGroup**, and in the search results, click **HomeGroup**.
- Click **Create homegroup.**

- Click **Next**.

- Choose what to share and click **Next**.

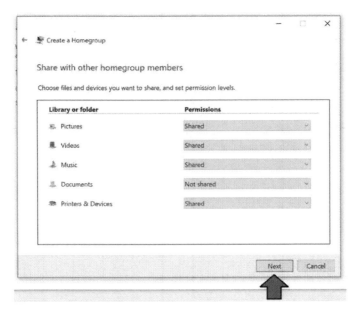

- Windows now displays a complex password, like W3fgsTg5jR. Copy this password or write it down. You also have the option to print the password. Click **Finish** when you are done.

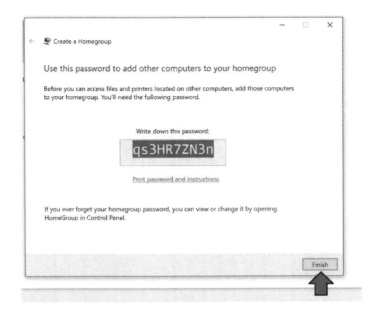

Joining a Homegroup

- On your second device/PC, open the HomeGroup panel just as you did in the section above (Please make sure you have the wireless on your device/PC connected to the same network as the one above).

- Click **Join homegroup/Join Now**

- Click **Next.**

- Choose what to share and click **Next.**

- Enter the password you copied above and click **Next**.

- Click **Finish** when you are done.

Tip:

To leave a Homegroup, select the search box in the Taskbar, enter **HomeGroup**, and in the search results, click **HomeGroup**. Then click on **Leave the homegroup...**

In addition, you can change what you share by clicking on **Change what you're sharing with the homegroup** (see the first option above).

If you are having problem connecting to a HomeGroup, make sure that the **Make this PC discoverable** feature is switched on. This will allow you to join/create a HomeGroup. To switch on this feature, go to **Settings > Network & Internet > Wi-Fi**. Click on the network you want to manage and then click the switch next to **Make this PC discoverable.**

Wi-Fi

Using your Surface, you can connect to the internet or other network devices anywhere an access point or wireless hotspot is available.

**To activate the Wi-Fi feature and connect to a network, do
these:**

1. Select the search box in the Taskbar, enter **WiFi**, and in the
 search results, select **Change Wi-Fi Settings**.

2. Click the switch next to **Wi-Fi** to turn it **On**. Your Surface
 will then automatically scan for networks. You may also
 manually add network. To manually add a network, select
 Manage known networks. Then select **Add a new
 network.**

3. If you see your network under the scanned networks, select
 it.

4. Enter a password for the network (if necessary).

To remove a saved Wi-Fi network:

1. Repeat step 1 above.
2. From the Wi-Fi settings screen, scroll to and click **Manage Wi-Fi Settings**.
3. Under **Manage known networks,** click the desired network that you want to remove.
4. Click **Forget.**

Hint: To prevent your Surface from connecting automatically to a network, repeat steps 1 and 2 mentioned above. Click on a network and select **Properties**. Tap the switch next to **Connect automatically when in range.**

Note:

- The Wi-Fi feature running in the background consumes battery. To save your battery, put it off whenever you are not using it.
- After you connect to a Wi-Fi network, your device should connect automatically to it again whenever that network is in range.

- The Wi-Fi may not connect to a network if the network signal is not very good.

- If your device cannot connect to a wireless network, check if the airplane mode is on/off. If the airplane mode is off, and you cannot still connect to a wireless network, try restarting your router or your Surface or both.

Tip: To disable all connections, turn **on** the **airplane mode** by swiping in from the edge of the screen and clicking on the **Airplane Mode**.

Using the Second Screen Option

You can connect your Surface to an external display like monitor or projector. This can be done wirelessly or by using a cable.

To connect your Surface to a wired display:

- Connect an HDMI/VGA cable to the HDMI/VGA port on your monitor, TV or projector. In addition, if your monitor has a DisplayPort, you can connect it to your Surface using a DisplayPort to Mini DisplayPort cable.
 If you are using VGA cable, you may need to use it with the Mini DisplayPort to VGA Adapter. A VGA adapter or cable is for video only and may not give any audio output.

- Connect the other end of the cable to a Mini DisplayPort on your Surface or Surface video adapter, or to the Mini DisplayPort on Surface docking stations (sold separately).

Please note that you may need to buy the cables mentioned above separately.

The Mini DisplayPorts on Microsoft Surface Pro and Microsoft Surface Laptop are shown below.

To connect your Surface to an external display wirelessly:

1. On your Surface, swipe in from the right edge of the screen to access Action Center.

2. Tap **Connect**, and in the list of displays, select the name of the wireless display you want to connect with.

Surface Dock and Microsoft Surface Pro/Microsoft Surface Laptop

Surface Dock (sold separately) allows you to connect many peripherals to Microsoft Surface Pro or Microsoft Surface Laptop.

To use Surface Dock with Microsoft Surface Pro or Microsoft Surface Laptop:

1. Plug the AC end of the Surface Dock power adapter into an electrical outlet or power strip, and plug the other end into the power port on Surface Dock.

Power port

2. Using the cable provided, connect Surface Dock to the charging port of your Surface. Make sure you remove any attached accessories (except the memory card) from your Surface before you connect it to the Surface Dock.

3. Connect your peripherals to the appropriate ports on the Surface Dock. Please make sure that you plug each cable to the right port on the Surface Dock.

Please note that you may need a Mini DisplayPort cable to connect a monitor to Surface Dock.

Access More By Using Bluetooth

Bluetooth option allows you to connect to another Bluetooth device within a close range.

Note: If there are obstacles such as a thick wall, the operating distance of the Bluetooth may be reduced.

To use Bluetooth feature:

1. Select the search box in the Taskbar, enter **Bluetooth**, and in the search results, select **Bluetooth and other devices settings**.
2. Then click the switch next to **Bluetooth.** Your Surface will then automatically scan for Bluetooth devices.
3. Click the device you want to connect to, and click **Pair**.
4. If the other device needs a passcode, type in or accept the passcode. If you don't know the code, you may try using 0000.

Please make sure that the device you are trying to connect with has its Bluetooth turned on and is discoverable. If you have problem connecting with a Bluetooth device, try restarting your Surface.

Tip: To share an item using Bluetooth, right-click on the item and select **Send to**. Then choose **Bluetooth device**. You will need to turn on Bluetooth to send items.

Location Services

Enabling location service allows Map and some other apps to serve you content related services.

Note: You may have to activate location service in order to use Cortana maximally.

To Activate Location Services:

1. Swipe in from the right edge of the screen to open the action center menu, and then click **All Settings.**

2. Click on **Privacy**.

3. Click **Change** next to **Location for this device is on** and select **On**. In addition, under **Location service**, select **On.**

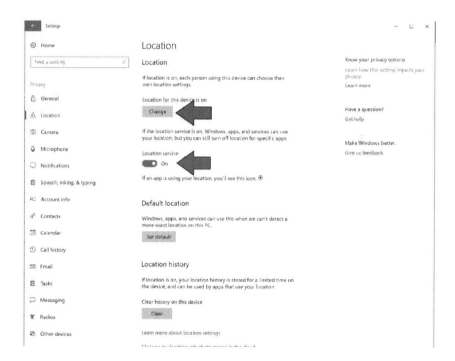

4. To choose the apps that can use your location, under **Choose apps that can use your location**, select the apps you want.

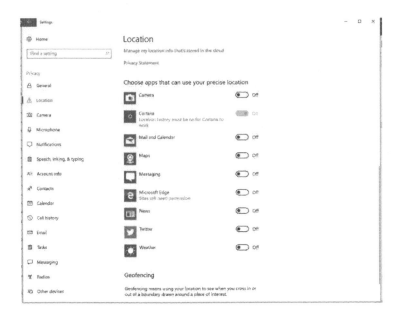

Settings

Settings menu gives you the opportunity to customize your device as you like.

To access the settings menu

1. Swipe in from the right edge of the screen to open the Action center menu and then click on **All Settings.**
2. Alternatively, you can click the Windows icon on the Taskbar and then click **Settings**.

The following are options under the Settings tab:

System

This option allows you to access displays, notifications, and power/battery settings.

Devices

Device settings gives you the opportunity to manage Bluetooth, printers and mouse settings.

Network & Internet

This option allows you to connect to Wi-Fi network, access the internet or other network devices and manage cellular settings.

Personalization

This option allows you to customize your device in a unique way.

Apps

This option allows you to manage the apps installed on your Surface.

Accounts

This option allows you to manage your Microsoft account, email account(s), and more.

Time & language

Use this option to control the time, keyboard, and language settings on your device.

Ease of Access

This option allows you to manage accessibility feature on your device. For more information on this, please refer to preceding chapter on **Accessibility** (see page 193).

Privacy

Use this setting menu to manage privacy settings on your device.

Update & security

Use this option to manage Windows update on your device.

What You Must Know About Your Microsoft Surface Pro/Microsoft Surface Laptop

Differences between Microsoft Surface Pro and Microsoft Surface Laptop

The main differences between Microsoft Surface Pro and Microsoft Surface Laptop are tabulated below.

	Microsoft Surface Pro	Microsoft Surface Laptop
Body size	11.50 x 7.93 x 0.33 inches	12.13 x 8.79 x 0.57 inches
Operating System	Windows 10 Pro	Windows 10 S (Upgradable to Windows 10 Pro)
Processor	7th-gen Core M/i5/i7 Intel Core processors	7th-gen Core i5/i7 Intel Core processors
Pixel Density	267	201

Touchscreen	Yes	Yes
Battery	Up to 13.5 hours depending on the usage	Up to 14.5 hours depending on the usage
Keyboard	Sold Separately	Included

How to Upgrade from Windows 10 S to Windows 10 Pro

If you are using Microsoft Surface Laptop, you will notice that you cannot install applications from third party stores. For you to install apps on your Surface laptop, you have to go to Windows store. The main reason you cannot do this is that Surface Laptop is running Windows 10 S.

If you want to upgrade to Windows 10 Pro from Windows 10 S follow the instructions:

Note: *Please note that you may not be able to go back to Windows 10 S after this upgrade. Please consider this before you upgrade.*

1. Download an app from a store other than Microsoft store. For example, you may attempt to download **Open Office** from openoffice.org.

2. After the download, click on the file to install it on your Surface laptop.

3. A dialogue box should appear telling you that your device OS only runs verified apps. At the bottom of the dialogue box, you should see a link telling you what to do. Click on the link to get started.

The upgrade should not take much time, and you should be able to install apps from stores other than Microsoft store after the upgrade.

Notes:

Make sure you save and close all your apps and files before initiating the upgrade.

Depending on some conditions, you may need to pay 49 dollars for the upgrade or you may be allowed to upgrade free. If you do not see the option to upgrade free then you don't meet the conditions for free upgrade and you will need to pay money to upgrade.

How to take screenshot on your Surface

Another task you can perform on your device is taking a screenshot. To take a screenshot with your device, please follow the instructions below:

Method 1

1. Navigate to the required page (the page you want to take its screenshot).
2. Hold the power button down and then press the volume up button.
3. To locate your screenshots, go to **Pictures**, and then click **Screenshots**.

Method 2

This is probably the simplest method. All you need to do to take a screenshot is to press the **Windows logo key + F8**. To locate your screenshots, go to **Pictures**, and then click **Screenshots**.

Please note that the **Fn** Key must be switched off for this to work. To know whether the **Fn** key is switched off or not, see whether the small light on the key is on. To switch **Fn** key off, just press the key once.

Windows key

Fn Key

Method 3

1. Select the search box in the taskbar, enter **Snipping tool**, and in the search results, tap **Snipping tool**.

2. Click the small dropdown arrow next to **Mode** and select an option.

a. **Free-form Snip**: This option allows you to capture a screenshot by moving the cursor in any direction.

b. **Rectangular Snip**: This option allows you to capture a screenshot by drawing a rectangular box on the area of the screen that you want to capture.

c. **Windows Snip**: This option allows you to capture a screenshot by clicking on a window on the screen.

d. **Full-screen Snip:** This option allows you to capture all what is on the screen.

3. When you have selected an option, click on **New** (you may also press **Ctrl + N**) and then click or move/drag the cursor round the area you want to capture.

Tip: If you love this tool and you will love to be using it, then I will advise that you pin it to the Taskbar for easy access. To do this, open the tool and right click on its icon on the Taskbar. Then select **Pin to taskbar.**

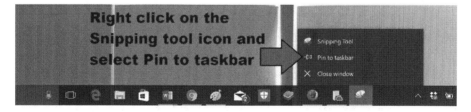

Method 4

Double-click the top button of your Surface pen to take a screenshot and write on it.

How about Finding Your Surface in case of lost

As a human being, it is not impossible that you misplace your Surface. If you are unable to find your Surface, Microsoft can help you locate it.

1. Go to **https://account.microsoft.com/devices**
2. Sign in if needed.
3. Click on **Find My Device** under your device's name. Then use the onscreen map to search for your Surface. Unfortunately, as at the time of writing this guide, there appears to be no way to make your Surface ring using this feature.

Please note that your Surface's Wi-Fi has to be turned on for you to know the location of it. In addition, **Find My Device** feature must be turned on before the device gets lost.

To turn on Find My Device feature:

Select the search box in the Taskbar, enter **Find My Device**, and in the search results, select **Find My Device**. Then check if it is turned on.

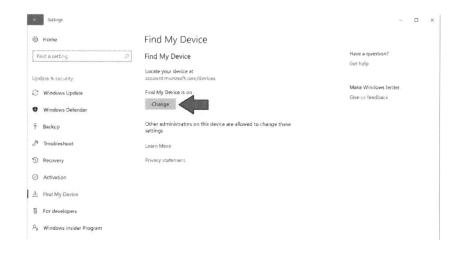

Solution to Non-Responding Apps

Sometimes an app may start misbehaving and may even refuse to close. If this happens, please try the following:

1. Swipe in form the left edge of the screen to access opened apps.
2. Locate this particular app, and Click on **X** icon to close it.

If the app does not close then try this:

Press **Ctrl + Alt + Delete** at the same time. This will bring out a list of items to pick from. Select **Task Manager** from the list to access the opened apps on your Surface.

Then right click on the app you want to close, and select **End task**.

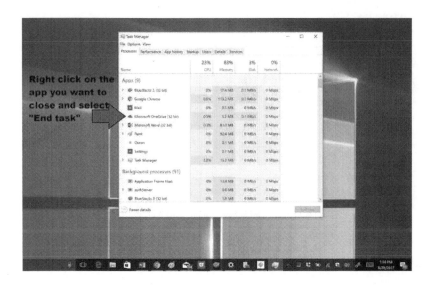

Alternatively, you can right click on the ^ icon located on the Taskbar to gain access to the Task Manager instead of pressing **Ctrl + Alt + Delete**.

Then, try launching the app again. If it is still misbehaving then you may try restarting your Surface.

How to Conserve Your Surface's Battery Life

You may notice that you have to charge your Surface twice a day in order to keep your Surface on. There are steps to follow to ensure that your Surface serves you throughout the day with just a single charge.

1. **Reduce the screen brightness:** I have realized over time that screen brightness consumes a lot of energy. There is usually a substantial difference between using a Surface with a maximum brightness and using it with a moderate brightness. As a rule, do not use your Surface with a maximum brightness unless you can't see what is on the screen clearly, for example, if you are outdoor, and please make sure you reduce it immediately when it is no more needed. To learn how to adjust screen brightness, please go to the **section on brightness** (see page 53).

2. **Shorten the Screen timeout:** If you really want to save your battery you must try to shorten the screen timeout. Reducing how long your Surface will stay lit up after you finish interacting with it will really help you to save battery. To manually put off the screen of your Surface, press the power button once.

 You can adjust the screen timeout settings by going to **Settings > System > Power & Sleep.**

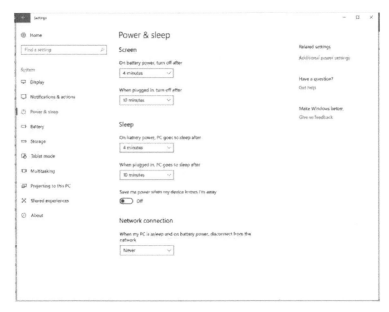

3. **Turn off Wi-Fi and Bluetooth:** When you are not using Wi-Fi or Bluetooth, please always remember to put them off. These features really consume energy and they are better off when not in use.

4. **Reduce number of notifications:** There are two benefits of doing this, the first is that there will be less distractions and the second benefit is that notification drains energy. Limit yourself to those notifications that are important to your life. To manage notifications, go to **Settings** > **System** > **Notifications & actions**.

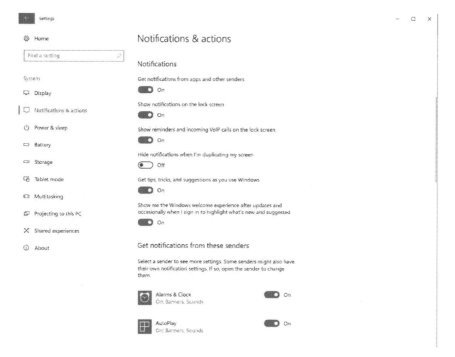

3. **Close all unnecessary apps:** The truth is that any app you
 open is using out of the limited battery energy. It is important
 to close any app you are not using from time to time. To
 access all apps currently running on your Surface, swipe in
 from the left edge of the screen to access the Task view and
 see all your open apps. Click on **X** icon to close any of the
 opened apps.

5. **Use a correct charger:** Using a wrong charger can endanger
 the health of your battery, and it is better to avoid such
 practice.

6. **Consider switching off your Surface:** If you are not going to use your Surface for an extended period, you may consider switching off your Surface.

7. **Use headphones:** Using the headphones is another cool way to save your battery. Extended use of audio speakers of your Surface may drain your battery faster. Please make sure you don't increase the volume of your audio too much while using headphones, as this may affect your ears.

Extras

Five ways of protecting your Surface with Windows Defender Security Center

Windows Defender is a Microsoft antivirus that comes with both Microsoft Surface Pro and Microsoft Surface Laptop. To access this antivirus, Select the search box in the Taskbar, enter **Windows Defender**, and in the search results, choose **Windows Defender Security Center**.

The five ways of protecting your Surface with Windows Defender are mentioned below:

1. Always make sure that your Windows Defender is updated to the most recent antivirus definition. Although Windows Defender should update itself automatically whenever there is a new virus definition and you are connected to the internet, I will still advise that you manually check for updates from time to time. This is important to make sure you don't miss any important update.

2. Always make sure you perform Windows Updates from time to time. You may want to ask that how does Windows update affect an antivirus? The truth is that there is a relationship between Windows Defender and Windows Update.

Sometimes, Microsoft upgrades the version of Windows Defender through Windows updates, but if you do not perform Windows updates on your system, how will you receive such an upgrade.

For example, some time ago, Microsoft released a Windows update for Windows Defender. According to Microsoft, this particular update will revise the definition files that are used to detect viruses, spyware, and other potentially unwanted software. This is why you have to perform Windows update from time to time.

Note: Unless you set your internet connection to be a **metered connection** (see page 290-293), Windows update should automatically be downloaded to your Surface when they are available and you are connected to a Wi-Fi.

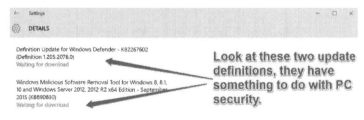

3. Perform a full system scan once a week. It is important to know the status of your PC. You can always perform a full PC scan by opening the Windows Defender app and clicking on **Virus & threat protection > Advanced scan > Full scan > Scan now**.

4. Scan any external storage device connected to your PC before using it. Although Windows Defender should automatically scan a connected external storage device, I will still advise that you manually scan an external device whenever you connect it to your PC. This is especially important if you don't trust the external storage device. Remember, the few minutes you use to scan an external storage device may save you some headaches in the nearest future.

5. Use Windows Defender with Windows Firewall for maximum security. Windows firewall protects your PC against unsafe apps or software from the internet or a network. Firewall informs you whenever unknown or malicious software wants to make changes to your Surface. Firewall is On by default, but you can still check it to be sure. To quickly check if it is on, type **Windows Firewall** into the search bar on the Taskbar and click on **Windows Firewall**. Then check if **On** is displayed next to Windows Firewall.

How to Change Your PC Name and Start screen name

In this section of the guide, I have carefully highlighted the steps to follow to get a change in user name or Start Screen name on your Surface.

Note: PC name is the name that is shown to other devices when they want to connect/pair with you. For example, a nearby Bluetooth device will see you as "Example" if you have given your PC that name.
On the other hand, your Start screen name is the name that appears on your Start screen when you wake your Surface from sleep.

There are many ways to initiate the PC/Surface name change, but I will talk about the one I prefer most.

To change the name of a PC/Surface:
1. Swipe in from the right edge of the screen and click on **All Settings**.

2. Click on **System.**

3.Click on **About** (the last item on the list)

4. Then click on **Rename PC** (as shown above).

5. Fill in the new name and click **Next.**

6. Then choose whether to restart now or later.

7. After restarting your PC/Surface, the name of your PC/Surface would have changed and electronic devices/gadgets will begin to see your PC/Surface bearing the new name you just changed to.

To change the Start screen name:

1. Press **Windows logo Key + R**

2. Type in **lusrmgr.msc** and press OK

3. Click on **Users.**

4. Then double click on the User name you want to change

5. Enter the new name and press **OK**

You may need to restart your PC before the changes appear.

Tip:

In addition, if you don't want to change the Start screen's name but still wants a new name on your start screen, you may consider creating a new account.

To create a new account, go to **Settings > Accounts > Family & other users**. Then click on **Add a family member/Add someone else to this PC**. After creating the account, click on it and select **Change account type**.

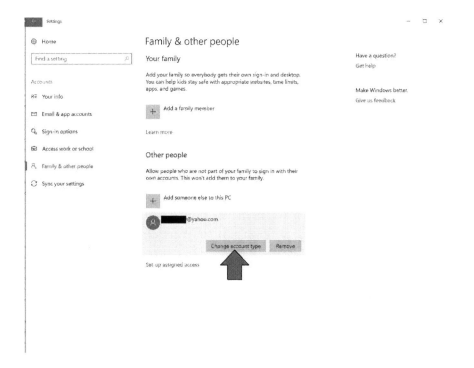

Click on the dropdown box and select **Administrator**.

Click **OK**.

Please note that making the new account an Administrator account will make it has an unrestricted access to most (if not all) the functions on the Surface.

How to avoid automatic Windows Update in Surface Pro and Surface Laptop

Since Surface Pro and Surface Laptop are running Windows 10, it is most likely that Windows updates get automatically downloaded to your device. If you will like to avoid this automatic windows update, there is way out. This is achieved by setting up metered connection. Doing this will let you avoid automatic updates and save some data.

To set up metered connection:
1. Go to Wi-Fi icon usually located at the lower bottom of the screen and click on it.
2. Click on **Network & internet settings.**

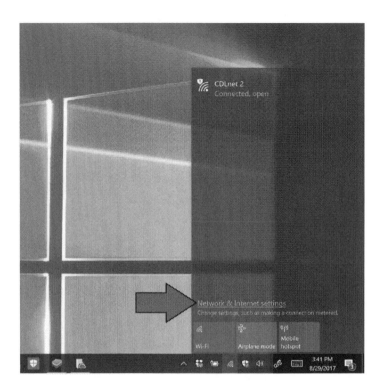

3. Click on **Change connection properties.**

4. Toggle the slider below **Set as metered connection** to On position.

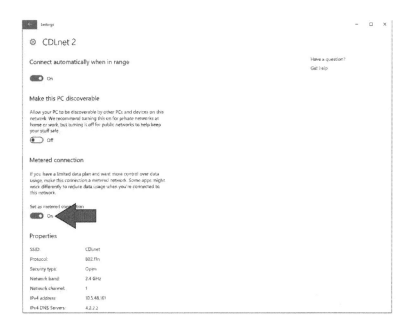

Safety Precautions When Using Your Surface on Wi-Fi

With many free Wi-Fi hotspots, it is likely that you are going to find yourself using Wi-Fi more on your Surface. There are few things to keep in mind when using Wi-Fi.

1. **Confirm the Network Name.**

Hackers sometimes set up a fake Wi-Fi network in order to access the information of unwitting public users. To avoid this, make sure you are sure of the name of the network you are connecting to. You may ask any trusted individual around you if you doubt the name of a network.

2. **Connect to a Secured Site.**

Whenever you are sending sensitive information always make sure that the site is a secured website. You can know whether a website is a secured one or not by checking whether the URL address of the website starts with **HTTPS.** If it starts with https and the certificate has not expired, then it should be a secured site.

3. **Get a Virtual Private Network (VPN)**

It is highly important you use a virtual private network when using a public network. There are both free and paid VPN providers.

4. **Avoid Automatic Connection**

Make sure your Wi-Fi is off when not using it to avoid your Surface automatically connecting to an open network. Turning your Wi-Fi off when not using it will also save your battery energy.

Troubleshooting

If the touch screen responds slowly or improperly or your Surface is not responding, try the following:

- Remove any protective covers (screen protector) from the touch screen.
- Ensure that your hands are clean and dry when tapping.
- Press the power button once to lock the screen and press it again to unlock the screen and enter a PIN/password if required.
- Try restarting your Surface.

Your Surface Doesn't Charge

- Make sure you are using Microsoft recommended charger to charge your Surface.
- If your Surface does not indicate that it is charging, unplug the power adapter and then restart your device.

Forgot Lock Screen Password or PIN

1. Using another device, visit **account.live.com** and log in with your registered email account. Please make sure you sign in with the same email address as on your Surface.
2. Click on **Forget my password.**
3. Follow the onscreen instructions to reset your password, then try signing into your Surface using your new password. Please make sure you are connected to internet while trying to log into your Surface.

Your device is hot to the touch

When you use applications that require more power or use applications on your device for a long period of time, your Surface may be a bit hot to touch. This is normal and it should not affect performance. You may just allow your Surface to rest for some time or close some applications.

Your Surface is not responding to touch

Try restarting your device. To force your Surface to shut down, long press the power button. Please note that you may lose your unsaved items if you shut down your Surface by force.

Surface does not connect Wi-Fi

Make sure you don't have limited network connectivity in that area. If your network is good and you still cannot connect, you may perform any of these actions:

- Make sure your Airplane Mode is off.
- Try restarting the Wi-Fi settings.
- Move closer to your router and scan for the available networks. If the network still does not show up, you may add the **network manually** (see page 255).
- Restart your router and modem. Unplug the modem and router for few minutes and plug the modem in and then the router.
- Try restarting you Surface.

Another Bluetooth device is not located

- Ensure Bluetooth feature is activated on your Surface and the device you want to connect to.

- Ensure that your Surface and the other Bluetooth device are within the maximum Bluetooth range.

Safety precautions

A. To prevent electric shock, fire, and explosion

1. Do not use damaged power cords or plugs, or loose electrical sockets.

2. Do not touch the power cord with a wet hand.

3. Do not bend or damage the power cord.

4. Do not short-circuit the charger.

5. Do not use your Surface during thunderstorm.

6. Do not dispose your Surface by putting it in fire.

B. Follow all safety warnings and regulations when using your device in restricted areas.

C. Comply with all safety warnings and regulations regarding mobile device usage while operating a vehicle.

D. Proper care and use of your Surface

1. Keep your Surface dry. Your Surface is not water resistant.

2. Do not use or store your Surface in hot or cold areas. It is recommended to use your device at temperature from 5^0C to 35^0C.

3. Do not put your Surface near magnetic fields.

4. When cleaning your Surface, do not use chemicals or detergents. You may use small towel.

5. Keep your Surface away from small children because they may mistakenly damage it. It may look like a toy to them.

Thanks for reading my guide, if you will like to contact me on anything, please send me an email at

pharmibrahimguides@gmail.com

You may also visit my author's page at

www.amazon.com/author/pharmibrahim

And please don't forget to follow me when you visit my author's page, just Click on **Follow** button located below the profile picture.

43196395R00172

Made in the USA
Middletown, DE
21 April 2019